planning a trip to Kyoto, or remembering past Gion Festival adventures, you'll find this volume full of invaluable insights into this portal to the past.

—Rebecca Teele Ogamo, Senior Director,
International Noh Institute

For the first time in English the extraordinarily rich heritage of Kyoto's premier festival is here given the coverage it deserves.

—John Dougill, author, *Kyoto, A Cultural History*

Happily, Catherine Pawasarat has now blessed us with a highly enjoyable guide to Gion Matsuri, that provides a thorough overview of this unique festival: its traditions, its roots, its rituals, its significance, and the unique system of community collaboration that has kept the festival going for more than 1,150 years.

The book has two main aspects. On the one hand it is a handy and practical guide book that you can carry around with you as you tour the festival. On the other hand, this book is also an initiation into the deeper significance of the festival. Pawasarat is a long-time teacher of Buddhist meditation techniques and her spiritual training has led her to some profound insights about the nature of this annual celebration.

Pawasarat also pays tribute to the local community that supports Gion Matsuri and lists the many innovative ways that they are adapting to the challenges of the modern era. Reading of the festival's transformation through the ages, the meaning behind each of its processions, and the sheer effort that goes into putting it on each year, one cannot fail to be impressed.

I enjoyed this book immensely. It is a treasure trove of information about the festival and beautifully illustrated with the author's own color photographs.

—Michael Lambe, writer, *DeepKyoto.com*

The author first encountered Gion Matsuri in her Kyoto neighborhood around 1990. Over many years, she has forged close bonds with local residents in chōnai associations, gradually absorbing their oral heritage while observing the impact of significant societal shifts.

The purpose of this book is clearly to raise awareness and appreciation of the unique value of this tradition, as a way of contributing to its long-term survival. A wealth of information is provided on its history, associated events, and how to access specific sites where individual floats and their treasures can be viewed up close in truly astounding detail. Descriptions of their sumptuous decorations may inspire even long-term residents to revisit with fresh eyes. ... Providing comprehensive descriptions never previously available in English, it is an invaluable aid to personal exploration. Its maps are detailed, as is the events schedule, and links are provided to a companion website, including YouTube videos.

—Kyoto Journal

Praise for *The Gion Festival: Exploring Its Mysteries*

The Gion Festival is the most important annual traditional event in Japan – and one of the richest cultural celebrations anywhere in the world. Yet until now there has never been a book devoted to it in English. Catherine Pawasarat's book, a labor of love involving decades of experience and research, will remain for many years to come as the definitive guide to the Gion Festival.

In heartfelt, easily accessible writing, Pawasarat introduces and explains every aspect of the festival: its history from earliest days through the 15th century Onin War, the decorative flair as well as the destructive fires of the Edo period, and its renaissance since the late 20th century; the design, symbolism, and treasures of each float; the neighborhoods and houses among which the festival takes place; the many religious rituals, parades, and musical performances that accompany it; as well as practical help in the form of photographs, schedules, and maps.

Pawasarat's writing brings the Gion Festival vividly to life. For those who plan to see the Gion Festival in the future, this book will provide critical background and information that was never available before.

—Alex Kerr, author, *Another Kyoto*

At long last, the spiritual, communal, and artistic facets of the magnificent Gion Matsuri are plainly explained in this comprehensive guidebook. The book is much more than this though—it is also a passionate argument for how communities might maintain their cultural traditions in the face of modernity. The author's personal knowledge and deep commitment to the sustainability of the festival places this guidebook in ground-breaking territory.

—John Einarsen, Founding Editor, *Kyoto Journal*

With background stories on the historical and religious roots of the festival, and detailed information on each individual yamaboko float, as well as links to interactive maps, Pawasarat's guide to the Gion Festival is a must-have for anyone traveling to Kyoto for the summer festivities.

—Marc Peter Keane, garden designer, author of *Japanese Garden Notes*

I grew up immersed in the traditional world of Kyoto culture. But Catherine's book showed me a whole new perspective of the Gion Matsuri that I had never known before.

—Yuka Tsuen, President, Tsuen Tea International, 24th generation green tea purveyor

The Gion Festival is more than a major summer event in Japan. It's a trip back in time with a fascinating international history. Full of details and practical information, this very accessible guide is the perfect companion to assure you'll discover new depths and intriguing mysteries of the festival. The author's love for the people and traditions of the festival and her passion for its importance to our world today are infectious. Whether you are an armchair traveler,

THE GION FESTIVAL
Exploring Its Mysteries

Catherine Pawasarat
Foreword by Diane Durston

Please visit GionFestival.org for my interactive maps.

© Copyright Catherine Pawasarat, 2020

The Gion Festival: Exploring Its Mysteries is licensed under the Creative Commons **Attribution-ShareAlike 4.0 International License (CC BY-SA 4.0)**. To view a copy of this license, visit http://creativecommons.org/licenses/by-sa/4.0/

Or mail a request to:
Creative Commons, P.O. Box 1866,
Mountain View, CA 94042, USA.

You are free to:

Share — copy and redistribute the material in any medium or format

Adapt — remix, transform, and build upon the material for any purpose, even commercially.

The licensor cannot revoke these freedoms as long as you follow the license terms. Under the following terms:

Attribution — You must give appropriate credit, provide a link to the license, and indicate if changes were made. You may do so in any reasonable manner, but not in any way that suggests the licensor endorses you or your use.

ShareAlike — If you remix, transform, or build upon the material, you must distribute your contributions under the same license as the original.

No additional restrictions — You may not apply legal terms or technological measures that legally restrict others from doing anything the license permits.

All text and images by Catherine Pawasarat.
Image consultant: Hon Tong "Bat" Fung.
Proofreading/editing: Richard Sadowsky.
Publishing wizard: Christopher Lawley.
Marketing ninja: Gazelle Antasuda.
Book design and formatting: JETLAUNCH.

First Printing, July 2020.

Ebook ISBN: 978-0-9985886-6-7
Paperback ISBN: 978-0-9985886-9-8

GionFestival.org

Also by the author:

Wasteland to Pureland: Reflections on the Path to Awakening
Co-authored with Doug Duncan

Dedicated to the deities of the Gion Festival and to all those who honor them.

*Thus shall you think of all this fleeting world:
A star at dawn, a bubble in a stream;
A flash of lightning in a summer cloud,
A flickering lamp, a phantom, and a dream.*

*—The Perfection of Wisdom Sutra
That Cuts Like a Thunderbolt,
a.k.a. The Diamond Sutra*

TABLE OF CONTENTS

Foreword.................................xvii
Preface...................................xxi
Acknowledgments.........................xxv
Introduction............................xxxiii

Gion Festival Overview......................1
  How to Use This Book...................4
    Gion Festival's Global Relevance Today......7

Brief History of the Gion Festival.............9
  Goryō-e: Making Peace with Angry Spirits......10
  When Did the Gion Festival
  Take Its Modern Form?...................12
  What About the Gion Festival Today?........16

Gion Festival's Spiritual Roots................20
  Yasaka Shrine: The God of Storms and
  Goddess of Rice 20
    Chimaki................................22
  The Ox-Headed Emperor..................23
    Here Be Dragons.......................25
      The Shinkōsai Procession.............26
      Chigo, Remnants of Child Mediums.....27
    Who's Who in the Portable
    Mikoshi Shrines........................27

The Kankōsai Procession	29
The Performing Arts	30
Pleasing the Gods	31
And Still More Gods	32

Community: The Gion Festival *Chōnai* 33

Stepping into the Challenge 39
Who is in the Gion Festival Community? 43
Women in the Gion Festival 44

Art Treasures 50

Architecture 55
Textiles 55
Music 59
Byōbu Matsuri 61

Visiting the Gion Festival 63

Enjoying Your Visit.....................64
Planning Your Visit.....................65
  Yasaka Shrine 66
    Omukae Chōchin Lantern Procession.....66
    Mikoshi Arai Portable Shrine
    Purification..........................67
    Shinkōsai: The Deities' Good Fortune
    Procession..........................68
    Kankōsai: The Return Good Fortune
    Procession..........................69
    Hanagasa Junkō: The Flower Umbrella
    Procession..........................69
  Yamaboko Floats 71

Explorations: What to See and Do
at the Gion Festival 73
  Float Construction: *Yamaboko Tate* 73
  Treasure Viewing. 76
  Byōbu Matsuri: Folding Screen Festival. 78
  Traditional Architecture: *Kyōmachiya*. 80
    Kaisho: Floats' Treasure Display Buildings. . . .81
      Architecture, Saki Matsuri (July 12-17). . .84
      Private Residences. 85
      Architecture, Ato Matsuri (July 19-24) . . .87
      Private Residences. 87
  Boarding Yamaboko 88
    Boarding Floats During the Saki Matsuri
    (July 13-16) 89
    Boarding Floats During the Ato Matsuri
    (July 19-24) 90
  Hikizome: Pull a Yama or Hoko. 90
    Saki Matsuri *Hikizome* 90
    Ato Matsuri *Hikizome*. 91
  Tea Ceremony. 92
  Dance and Music 92
  Noh Theater 96
  Museums. 96
  Kyoto's Massive Historic Street Parties:
  Yoiyoiyoiyama, Yoiyoiyama, and Yoiyama. 97

The *Yamaboko* Floats. 99
  Yama and Hoko Floats Explained 100

Saki Matsuri: The "Early Festival:" July 10-17....103
  The Saki Matsuri Timeline: Overview........104
    The Saki Matsuri floats procession........106
      Tsuji Mawashi Corner Turning........109
  Abura Tenjin Yama 油天神山:
  The Oil Thunder-Deity Float............114
  Arare Tenjin Yama 霰天神山:
  The Hail Thunder-God Float............117
  Ashikari Yama 芦刈山:
  The Reed Cutter: Love Reunited...........120
  Ayagasa Boko 綾傘鉾:
  The Damask Umbrella Float..............123
  Fune Boko 船鉾: The Ship Float...........127
  Hakuga Yama 伯牙山:
  Understanding through Sound............131
  Hakurakuten Yama 白楽天山:
  Zen—Simply Profound..................134
  Hōka Boko 放下鉾:
  The Renunciate's Float.................137
  Hoshō Yama 保昌山: Courageous Love.......141
  Iwatō Yama 岩戸山: The Stone Door Float....144
    Lighting Up the Heavens...............145
  Kakkyō Yama 郭巨山: Confucian and
  Taoist Teachings......................148
  Kankō Boko 函谷鉾: The Valley Pass Float....151
    China's Famous Kankō (Han Gu) Pass.....152
  Kikusui Boko 菊水鉾:
  The Chrysanthemum Water Float..........155
  Mōsō Yama 孟宗山:
  Confucian Teachings on Family...........158

Naginata Boko 長刀鉾: The Long Sword Float .161
　The *Chigo*, Vestige of Child Mediums 161
Niwatori Boko 鶏鉾: Dedicated to Peace. 165
Shijō Kasa Boko 四条傘鉾:
An Umbrella and Children's Dance 169
Taishi Yama 太子山: Japan's Saintly Genius. . . .172
Tokusa Yama 木賊山:
Father and Son Reunited. 175
Tōrō Yama 蟷螂山: Brave as a Mantis 178
Tsuki Boko 月鉾: The Moon Float 181
Urade Yama 占出山: Empress Jingū Divines
The Future 185
Yamabushi Yama 山伏山:
Buddhist Nature Mystics. 188

The Ato Matsuri: The "Later Festival"
July 18-24. 191
　What's the Ato Matsuri Timeline?. 193
　　The Ato Matsuri Floats Procession 196
　En-no-Gyōja Yama 役行者山:
Shugendō's Founder 199
Hachiman Yama 八幡山:
Protector of Warriors. .202
Hashi Benkei Yama 橋弁慶山:
Loyalty and *The Tale of the Heike*. 205
Jōmyō Yama 浄妙山:
Incredible Warrior Monks 208
Kita Kannon Yama 北観音山:
Northern Kannon Float. 211
Koi Yama 鯉山: The Carp That Became
A Dragon 215

Kuronushi Yama 黒主山: An Immortal Poet . . . 219
Minami Kannon Yama 南観音山:
The Southern Kannon Float 223
    Kyōmachiya and Architectural
    Conservation 225
Ōfune Boko 大船鉾: The Great Ship Float 227
    The Restoration of Ōfune Boko 228
Suzuka Yama 鈴鹿山:
The Demon-Pacifying Goddess. 231
Taka Yama 鷹山: The Falconry Float 235

Practical Tips. 239
    Before You Go. 239
    Once You're There. 242

Schedule 245
Maps. 275
Afterword 281

FOREWORD

As an 18-year resident of Kyoto and the author of two books about the city myself, I was amazed (and very pleased) a few years ago to encounter someone who was writing a detailed book about Gion Matsuri, one of the oldest and most complex urban festivals in the world. I knew from personal experience of the many challenges faced by anyone attempting to enter the tightly knit, tradition-bound Kyoto society—a world difficult to understand even for Japanese from outside the city.

As the old imperial capital of Japan, Kyoto was the heart of the development of Japanese culture and history for more than a thousand years. From Shintō to Buddhism, literature, music, and architecture to the tea ceremony with the myriad of exquisitely handmade ceramics, lacquerware, and bamboo crafts that support it, Kyoto was the stage on which much of the history of Japan played out over the centuries. It was here that Catherine Pawasarat succeeded in gaining the trust of the multi-generational leaders of the festival's *yamaboko* floats' neighborhoods, the keepers of Kyoto's revered Gion Matsuri.

Her book provides us now with a well-researched and thoughtful English-language survey of the many esoteric aspects of this complex festival. It offers the first-ever, comprehensive glimpse of the way in which a centuries-old festival has served as the glue that holds the fabric of this classical Japanese city together. Catherine's knowledge of language, passion for cultural understanding, and her facility for connecting with people across the cultural divide, enabled her to penetrate deeply into the heart of this 1200-year-old city, its magnificent festival, and the remarkable families that have carried on this rich tradition for generations.

Catherine came to this project with the language skills and unquenchable curiosity required to make a meaningful contribution to the ever-growing body of knowledge about Japan. Her commitment to studying both Japanese history and language opened the door for her to gather a depth of information and insight not often afforded to visiting journalists. Her genuine interest in every detail of the festival enabled her to learn first-hand from the many individuals involved in the festival and the dedicated community that fosters it.

The book is at once an insider's practical guide to seeing the festival in person and a compendium of detailed information about each of the 34 festival floats, including a set of indispensable maps to their neighborhoods and viewing locations.

More importantly, Catherine has provided us with an overview of the long history of the festival, its spiritual roots, and its significance to the community that has long kept its spirit alive. With sections that introduce the art, music, and architecture of the neighborhoods that support each float, the book also details many of the cultural activities and traditional art forms, such as the tea ceremony and Noh performances, that play an important role in the life of the city and events that surround the festival.

In 2018, I invited Catherine to co-curate an exhibition about Gion Matsuri in the Pavilion Gallery of the Portland Japanese Garden where I served as the Curator of Culture, Art, and Education for 12 years. Catherine's expertise in the intricacies of the festival enhanced the understanding of everyone who visited the exhibition, which featured the Ayagasa Boko, an authentic float from the festival, on its first journey outside of Japan, accompanied by a troupe of 20 *Gion bayashi* musicians from Naginata Boko float to perform the uniquely Kyoto style of festival music.

Now with this book, Catherine has created an authentic insider's look at the festival that will open the eyes and hearts of all who peruse its pages. Her book offers insights into the beauty and the spiritual and cultural significance of the festival, and in doing so, she unlocks some of the mysteries at the cultural heart of this 1200-year-old city itself.

Diane Durston
Author of *Old Kyoto,*
Kyoto: Seven Paths to the Heart of the City,
and *Wabi Sabi: The Art of Everyday Life.*

PREFACE

Quite by chance, I lived in the heart of the Gion Festival neighborhood during the early 1990s, bubble-era Japan, in a beautiful, historic home with an enormous garden. Traditional Kyoto homes—known as *kyōmachiya*—had fallen out of fashion. Japanese people were more interested in living a Westernized lifestyle, sitting on chairs rather than on *tatami*-mat floors, with modern conveniences like air conditioning and heating. But I was young and relatively new to Kyoto, and loved the charm and novelty of this cultural experience.

During this time, one hot, sticky July morning, I first encountered a Gion Festival float. The timber frames and wheels of what would become Kita Kannon Yama had suddenly appeared outside my front door. "What's this?" I asked the Japanese people standing around. "A *yama*," they said. Naturally, I responded, "What's a *yama?*"

"Men pull it through the streets during the procession," they answered. When I asked, "Why?" they paused, speechless, looking puzzled.

I kept asking, and that's how this book began, nearly 30 years and thousands of questions ago. I bow in homage to the Gion Festival community for their patience with me.

When I first encountered the Gion Festival, I was working as a journalist and translator, which helped me investigate it further. As time went by I undertook a meditation practice. Fast forward 20 years and now I teach Buddhist philosophy and meditation at a retreat center that I helped found and develop. This has helped me investigate it further too.

I was well along my spiritual path (or so I thought) when one particularly sultry Gion Festival night I found myself trapped in body-against-body crowds, wanting to escape. I felt desperately stuck amidst a clamor of humanity: chaotic sights of portions of street stalls and the backs of peoples' heads, the unpredictable movements of the crowd, and smells of bodies mixed with street food.

Though I couldn't move, part of me was flailing around, grasping for anything that could provide some solace. What caught my ear was the unearthly Gion Festival music: *kon chiki chin, kon chiki chin.* The rhythm, bell ringing, and flute notes came from all directions and no direction at the same time.

In that moment, space opened up and realization dawned: I was in the middle of a Shintō purification ritual, a contemporary ascetic practice.

That insight brought relaxation. My disquiet was replaced with a pervasive bliss. All of us in this madding crowd were in the same boat: trying to enjoy ourselves in conditions that made enjoyment nearly impossible. Understanding that we were suffering through it together helped me feel a strong communal bond with these countless strangers.

An entirely new dimension of the Gion Festival opened up after that. I started to notice how many smaller rituals were constantly going on within the massive ritual known as the Gion Festival. Goodness is ceaselessly invited in, while misfortune is repeatedly cast out from every direction.

As you will learn, the Gion Festival was begun in ancient times to placate angry spirits, believed to be the cause of widespread illness. Only in the 20th century did science reveal to Kyotoites that lack of sanitation combined with the city's annual summer rains, floods, and standing water to cause Kyoto's "summer sickness." By the 2000s, with diseases like cholera long absent from Kyoto, I wondered whether modern hygiene and infrastructure had made the Gion Festival's spiritual origins inapplicable, if not irrelevant.

But nowadays climate change has me thinking about prayers to Susano-o-no-Mikoto, the Japanese god of storms, in new ways. Floods struck Kyoto in July 2018, and death and destruction caused by record-breaking rainfall ensued in spite of modern engineering and science. I was planning to launch this book at Kyoto's Gion Festival in July 2020. As I was writing, the COVID-19 virus spread worldwide with astonishing speed. Most major Gion Festival events were canceled in 2020, almost unheard of in its millennium of history.

The irony is that the two main deities of the Gion Festival—Gozu Tennō, and Susano-o-no-Mikoto—are known as protectors from epidemics. The Gion

Festival was first held, we're told, to rid the city of a plague. Now I wonder: perhaps it was held to give thanks for surviving one.

Of course, the big question is, do gods and spirits actually exist? According to Buddhist philosophy and quantum physics, what we regard as a "self" does not inherently exist. So who can say?

But given the current challenges that humanity and the planet face, and the mysteries of how we can learn to live well together on this beautiful planet, it seems beneficial to invite the support of the unseen world.

Catherine Pawasarat, March 2020
Clear Sky Retreat Center
Fort Steele, B.C., Canada

ACKNOWLEDGMENTS

When I started to think about all the people who helped make this book possible, their numbers felt vast, like stars in space, as did their generosity. It's a nice feeling. I've used only parts of most people's names and omitted organization names in order to protect people's privacy.

To Namgyal Rinpoche, thank you for lighting the path.

Thank you, Acariya Doug Duncan, for ceaselessly, compassionately helping me learn to keep my heart and mind open. And making it fun. Among countless other things, I'm grateful for your ongoing support for my commitment to the Gion Festival.

To the deities of the Gion Festival, I pay my respects and give gratitude. Experiencing some of the mysteries of this world through my evolving relationship with you has nourished me.

To my parents and other ancestors, deep thanks for providing life and such an outstanding and supportive upbringing. Growing up with your guidance and support have helped make more wonderful things possible than you can know.

To the countless beings who have kept the Gion Festival going for more than 1150 years, I honor your amazing commitment, and I endeavor to help carry it into the future.

To Higuchi-san, thank you for introducing me to the world of traditional Japanese culture, Rokkaku-cho, and the Gion Festival. Our friendship is a treasure.

To Sakurai-san, you welcomed me when I knew no one, gave me a place to rest when I had none, and have shared so much. Thank you and may your kindness be repaid a thousand times. Special thanks also to Mrs. Sakurai for your kindness.

To all the yamaboko hozonkai members: I recognize your tireless and generous commitment. Thanks to you millions of us can enjoy the Gion Festival.

Because the Gion Festival is an "all-male festival," most of the Gion Festival people I've met and spent time with are men too. In some cases, I've gotten to know their wives, or other women who are involved. I'm embarrassed to say that it's taken me many years to perceive their different but equal commitment to the Gion Festival and Kyoto culture. Deep thanks and respect to all the women who support the Gion Festival from behind the scenes, and a special bow to those women (and the fathers, husbands, sons, and other men who support them) courageous enough to step out and support it in the front.

To Peter, thank you for your tireless encouragement, counsel, and artistic contributions. Your support helped me through some uncertain times. And thank you for introducing me to the lovely and fascinating ARC team at Ritsumeikan.

To G and Chris, your talents always amaze, encourage, and animate me. Without your support, this book wouldn't have been possible.

To the Planet Dharma and Clear Sky teams, what a pleasure it is to practice, live, and work with you. I appreciate you holding down the forts while I sequestered myself to write this book.

To Bat, huge thanks for your help with the innumerable images, software transfers, learning curves, and so on. Are you training to be a bodhisattva or something?

Richard, I appreciate your close and thoughtful reading and comments. Not many people could handle this challenge, and you did so admirably. I hear you get triple merit points when working overtime.

To Matsumiya-san, I've so enjoyed our time together. Thank you for devoting your artistic and other talents and historical research for others' benefit.

To Sakakibara-san, I'm so grateful for your patient assistance with my ever-improving Kyoto manners, and ceaselessly-evolving understanding of how to wear yukata and kimono. What would I do without you?

To Mr. and Mrs. Nasu, Kakimi, Okui, Yamamoto, Kobayashi, Tanimoto, Dejima, and Kishida, I'm grateful to you for welcoming me into your homes and hearts. It's been a tremendous pleasure to get to know you and your families. Meeting you each festival has become one of the things I most look forward to. Thank you for all you've shared with me.

Nasu-san, thank you for sharing so much with me about the history and culture of the Gion Festival, your float, and chōnai. Thanks to your generosity it's been delightful.

Nobuko, what a world you've introduced me to! I so respect and appreciate your commitment to sharing the origins of the Gion Festival textiles. I recognize your achievements and dedication, and applaud your ability to overcome systemic challenges.

Teraura-san, you are such a valuable member of the Gion Festival community. Thank you for letting me learn from your explorations and discoveries.

To the late Nagae-san, your commitment to the festival impressed me deeply. Your connection to Empress Jingu and onmyōdo opened up a magical world for me. May your beautiful home and memory benefit many for years to come. Mrs. Nagae, thank you for your support of this book.

To the Yoshidas, my heartfelt thanks for welcoming me into your world and your home. I hope that I may do you and your aesthetic and architectural conservation efforts justice. Your demonstration of how conservation and positive radicalism go together so well has been a great teaching for me.

To the late Oike-san, I feel grateful to you for demonstrating the incredible power of simply keeping an open mind, and investigating new perspectives.

To Diane Durston, thank you for understanding what I have been trying to do, and for inviting me to join you, your lovely team, and our wonderful friends from Naginata Boko and Ayagasa Boko at the beautiful Portland Japanese Garden. Your book *Old Kyoto* was a treasured resource while I lived in Kyoto.

To Hata-san, I've learned so much from your gracious hospitality and unique perspective on the Gion Festival. It's my sincere wish that many others may benefit from your wisdom, experience, and other resources.

Jeremy, thanks for sharing your incredible discoveries, insights, and adventures. It's been a treat to observe how what can seem like a mad fairy tale is actually authentic. I value your commitment to truth and courage to stand by your findings, all of which have been confirmed by other experts 25 years after you first said them.

To Gōtō Sensei, Fukami Sensei, Yagi Sensei, Kurotake-san, and Mr. and Mrs. Kitagawa, thank you for taking the time and energy to share your perspectives, knowledge, and experience with me. Thanks to you and other interviewees, we can appreciate the Gion Festival more than ever before.

Fukui-san, thank you for teaching me about some of the Gion Festival's most important traditions.

I felt moved by the late Ichihashi-san's gentle, steadfast dedication to community and tradition. Mrs. Ichihashi, I look forward to meeting again.

Yoshii-san, Yuko-san would be so happy to see us enjoying the fruits of our efforts today.

To Terakawa-san, Jōno-san, Torii-san, Furukawa-san, Kawazuka-san, Teranishi-san, Sanuki-san, Tanabe-san, Hasegawa-san, Watanabe-san, and Kawazoe-san, your kindness and generosity have brightened many a rainy day.

Shimotsuma Sensei, Aizawa-san, and Kato-san, thanks for your warm welcome and support. Kato-san, thanks for letting me know about my kimono and helping me fix it. A friend in need is a friend indeed.

To my friends at Ayagasa Boko, it's been a pleasure to get to know you better, and I look forward to more.

To my new friends at Naginata Boko, it's been lovely to have some time together. I appreciate your efforts to share the Gion Festival more internationally. I would love to do that together more often.

Linda, thank you for your beautiful hospitality, the pleasure of your company, and many delicious meals each summer.

Nakata-san, thank you for the book. I'd love to take photos of the festival together some time.

To the late Prof. Sugimoto, thank you for teaching me and illustrating that the most traditional Gion Festival people have also always been the most international! That made my head spin in a delightful way.

To Shimada-san and Nishiyama-san, a deep bow for all you've done to educate people about and share the beauty of the Gion Festival. Of course, I am still always learning from and studying your books! I feel fortunate that we've met and had some time together.

To Yamaguchi-san, Ueda-san, Taniguchi-san, and Kobayashi-san, thank you for your support and all the essential work you do for the Gion Festival.

Deep thanks to all of the Yamaboko Hozonkai representatives who gave me permission to use the photos of their floats in this book. I sincerely wish that what I've shared helps your chōnai, yamaboko, and the Gion Festival to thrive. And thank you for all you do for the hozonkai! Without your efforts, the Gion Festival wouldn't exist.

Big appreciation to Wada-san, for your tireless organization of countless festival volunteers.

THE GION FESTIVAL

Many thanks to all the *hikiko* and *kakite* for using their energy and strength to keep the floats moving. And round those corners!

I appreciate the *kurumakata* by the float wheels, the *yanekata* on the float roofs, and Kyoto police for helping keep everyone safe.

To the yamaboko carpenters: you guys are amazing. Thanks for keeping this important aspect of the tradition alive, safe, and beautiful to behold.

Sarah, thanks for kindly providing a place to stay.

Special thanks to David Kubiak and Donna Ward for finding The Big House and pursuing the incredible notion of us living there.

To Ken Rodgers, John Einarsen, Susan Pavlovska, Lucinda Cowing, and the rest of the *Kyoto Journal* team, thank you for your long-standing support. And for your beautiful publication.

To the kind and generous souls who wrote endorsements for this book: I appreciate you supporting my effort to share a generative message about the splendor of the Gion Festival with a more international audience.

To Nakamura-san, Ida-san, Miyoshi-san, and other friends from Kyoto Tsushinsha, what a lovely experience it has been to work together with you and get to know you over these years. I appreciate all your ongoing support for this book, and your outstanding festival parties.

Heartfelt thanks to Nakamura Masashi for introducing me to the very important framework of malevolent *onryō* spirits transforming into benevolent *goryō* deities.

Thanks to the late Morimoto-san for pointing out to me the link between Gozu Tennō and Yamantaka.

I appreciate Steven L. Renshaw's enthusiastic support regarding Japan's approach to astronomical constellations.

Lastly, special thanks to noh actress Rebecca Ogamo Teele for introducing me to the wondrous depths of noh theater.

INTRODUCTION

It gives me great pleasure to introduce you to Kyoto's spectacular Gion Festival, a precious gem among historic and cultural celebrations worldwide.

I was first mesmerized by the appearance of the Gion Festival, mostly its floats and their magnificent, diverse treasures. In the early 1990s, information in English was scarce. My speaking and reading of Japanese were pretty good, but many of the specialized Gion Festival words weren't listed in dictionaries.

So I pursued learning in one of the best ways: by listening to people who knew things. The Gion Festival neighborhood was and is notorious for being all-male and closed to outsiders, but I found community members to be very kind and generous. Festival elders, in particular, shared what they knew. Listening to them, my interest in the physical treasures was overtaken by my esteem for the community that has supported the Gion Festival for more than 1150 years.

Over time I noticed that it felt more rewarding to speak to some festival patrons than others. On reflection, I realized that people I enjoyed listening to seemed to feel a deep sense of meaning in connection with the festival. The meaning might vary—honoring the festival *kami* or deities, respecting the contributions of past festival patrons, awe for the tiny role we each play in a long and illustrious history, etc.—but spending time with them felt enriching, generative. When I spoke to them I felt nourished and revitalized.

This new interest in meaning catalyzed me to engage more with the significance *behind* the festival. What was it that kept this many people committed to the Gion Festival for so many centuries? Why did *chōnai* neighborhoods esteem the deities and treasures that they did? This book is designed to explore those questions.

Since the Gion Festival's 1150-plus years of history pre-date tourism, we can understand that it wasn't and isn't designed to be a tourist event in the typical sense. Event times and events themselves change from year to year. Clear schedules are hard to come by.[1] This must be a very ancient aspect of the psyche, when Japanese culture was more in accord with natural and fluctuating cycles of nature—before Japanese trains became so punctual that you could set your watch to their departure. At any rate, the moral of this tale is to go with the flow.

Speaking of going with the flow, the beautiful home and garden that I once lived in within the Gion Festival neighborhood have been knocked down and replaced with a large apartment building. A 250-year-old historic department store, Matsuzakaya,

---

[1] When I ask what time something will take place, it's not rare for the answer to be, "At the appropriate time."

had stood with great dignity next door when I lived there. In its place now is a new hotel.

Modern hotels and apartments supplanting historic buildings is an essential part of the contemporary Gion Festival experience. Ironically, people want to live and stay in the famous Gion Festival neighborhood. But this very desire is driving up real estate prices and taxes, making it impossible for families and companies with historic roots to stay. However welcome newcomers and visitors may be to the area, generally speaking, we new folks don't honestly know how to support the festival. Or even that it needs support. We're preoccupied with our own experience.

The basic challenge is this: contemporary approaches to tourism and real estate are based on a consumerist model. Whether we're aware of it or not, we're driven by considerations like, "What can I get?" "What can I experience?" "What can I take home with me?" In this regard, we modern people have a terrible habit of loving things to death, and the Gion Festival risks being one of those things. More and more visitors are wanting to get an experience that only a currently shrinking number of community members can offer.

It doesn't need to be this way. Whether you believe in Shintō rituals or not, if you are in the middle of an enormous ritual, on some level you are participating in it. Whether we are conscious of being in a community or not, if we are physically present in one, on some level we are a part of it. The choice of how we wish to participate is personal and reflects our sensitivity, our feeling of—or desire for—connection.

Tourism can be a force for positive change. Rather than acquiring objects and unique experiences, we can open ourselves to being transformed and feeling connected, which heightens our sense of wonder and brings new insights. This book is designed to facilitate such transformations.

I recognize that my perspective is very much that of a white American woman. I look forward to more diverse global and racial perspectives joining in the conversation about the significance of the Gion Festival.

Each year I've gone to the Gion Festival I tried to visit and learn more about each float. However, as fate will have it, some people and floats I got to know better than others. I naturally ended up spending more time with people who had become friends. I've tried my best to provide an accurate balanced presentation of the Gion Festival, and apologize for my inevitable errors and shortcomings.

It has been a tremendous pleasure to get to know the Gion Festival and its community over the last 30 years. And once more I am delighted to welcome you to join us. It is my sincere desire that this book helps you to enjoy the richness and profundities of the Gion Festival's offerings.

GION FESTIVAL OVERVIEW

Within Kyoto's extraordinary Gion Festival, deities, myths, and legends intermingle with modern people and lifestyles, plus centuries of rich culture and history. The result is a unique, luxurious universe, a neverending story that we continue to co-create. The Gion Festival has long only been understood by a small community of insiders. This guidebook introduces the Gion Festival's magic and majesty to English speakers. Welcome.

One of Gion Festival's stunning mikoshi, *or portable shrines.*

The Gion Festival is a *Shintō* festival, and Shintō is Japan's indigenous spiritual tradition, a kind of animism or shamanism. It translates to "path of the spirits," and there are more than 80,000 Shintō shrines in the country. Abundant in deities, one proverb holds that Shintō honors eight million gods. In this way, Shintō is very spiritually open: it honors nature spirits, the spirits of some remarkable humans, as well as archetypal entities, not so different from Mayan, Yoruban, or Greek gods.

Gion Festival floats purify Kyoto streets in the July 24 Ato Matsuri procession.

Consequently, we can see spiritual practices all around us at the Gion Festival today. In many ways, it's an extensive, month-long purification ritual, including countless ceremonies and prayers to an array of supernatural beings from different spiritual traditions. In particular, the **Yasaka Shrine's** portable *mikoshi* shrines and the Gion Festival **yamaboko floats** purify the city streets, neighborhoods, and people, creating a space free from harmful spirits and the plagues and other misfortune they might bring.

And what are all the prayers for? A year of safety, health, and general protection from harm. In other words, the Gion Festival invites a year of goodness to Kyoto City, its residents, and visitors.

Though Japan often gets stereotyped as a homogenous country, it's very spiritually and culturally diverse. Japanese people and culture generally accept whatever works into their spiritual cosmography, and that brings varied cultural influences with it. Gion

THE GION FESTIVAL

Festival patrons were keen to impress the populace with their sophistication and exotic foreign treasures: in centuries gone by, artwork often referred to philosophy and literature. Look closely and you'll see signs of Shintō, Zen, Mahayana Buddhism, Taoism, Christianity, Judaism, Islam, and Greek mythology. In this sense, the Gion Festival shines as both one of Kyoto's longest-standing traditions as well as a remarkably international event.

*Chinese Taoist Immortals contemplate the yin- yang symbol in this textile at **Hoshō Yama**.*

Speaking of goodness, the Gion Festival is definitely also an opportunity for good fun. It's likely that most people at the Gion Festival are enjoying themselves in a worldly way, rather than having a particularly spiritual experience. And in a city with festivals year-round, the Gion Festival is Kyoto's most famous and popular celebration, generating prosperity for Kyoto

*Students at Ikenobo Junior College enjoying being next door to **Niwatori Boko**.*

City, Kyoto Prefecture, and the country. More than a million visitors come to the Gion Festival each year to see and be seen, sample the amazing street food, and be dazzled by the magnificent **floats** and portable *mikoshi* shrines.

How to Use This Book

Spending time at the Gion Festival over the years, I've noticed that more than half of non-Japanese visitors are not native speakers of English. I've written this book with that in mind.

The Gion Festival is so vast in scope that it may be helpful to have a general sense of it before learning about the details. That is where these orienting sections at the beginning of the book can be useful.

A pleasant stroll by ***Tokusa Yama.***

When a word or phrase is marked in bold, that means you can go to that section or pages elsewhere in the book. In the ebook, there are also hyperlinks to more information on other websites. Japanese people's names are given Japanese style, with the family name first.

The enormous Gion Festival is roughly divided into two parts. The first, more traditional portion centers around **Yasaka Shrine**, and the second, better-known branch focuses on the

THE GION FESTIVAL

yamaboko **floats**. Both observe the **Saki Matsuri** ("early festival") from July 10 to 17, and the **Ato Matsuri** ("later festival") from July 18 to 24. Each of these portions has its own section in this book.

Use this book while you walk around, referring to the relevant pages. For example, each **yamaboko float** has its own pages you can refer to as you explore neighborhoods downtown (begin at Shijō Karasuma subway station and use our **maps**[2] at the end of this book). The information presented here will help you to better understand what you're looking at and experiencing.

I got to know the Gion Festival by wandering around and chancing upon magical experiences. This is still my favorite way to enjoy the festival. During the **Saki Matsuri** (July 10-17),[3] the float neighborhoods in the south and west are quieter and more pleasant for strolling and sightseeing. The **Ato Matsuri** (July 18-24)[4] is also more accessible this way. July 15, 16 and 23 (called *yoiyoiyama* and *yoiyama*) are extremely crowded, and an unforgettable sensorial extravaganza. Walking around the **Yasaka Shrine** grounds and surrounding neighborhoods along the mountains is delightful at any time.

---

[2] Go to **GionFestival.org** to access my interactive maps to the Gion Festival.
[3] Large **float construction** begins July 10, while the smaller floats' construction starts and float **treasures** go on display from July 12.
[4] Large **float construction** begins July 18, and smaller floats' construction starts, and their **treasures** are on display from July 20.

The Yamaboko Floats procession on July 17.

During the days leading up to the processions, visitors can watch the ***yamaboko tate***, when communities re-create their **yamaboko floats** from the ground up and adorn them with priceless treasures. Check out the pages devoted to each float to get a sense of what the float and its ***chōnai* community** are like.

Walking between floats, keep your eyes open for cultural riches displayed as part of the ***Byōbu Matsuri*** (Folding Screen Festival) in private homes and companies.

The highlights of the Gion Festival are the marvelous processions on July 17th and 24th. On both mornings, grand processions of ***yamaboko* floats** grace the main roads of central Kyoto. These processions won recognition as a cultural World Heritage event by UNESCO in 2009.

On the same nights, the streets break out in more boisterous, vigorous spectacles. Countless men hoist three portable ***mikoshi*** shrines on their shoulders through the neighborhoods between Yasaka Shrine and their *otabisho* visiting place downtown in the **shinkōsai** and **kankōsai** processions.

THE GION FESTIVAL

On the morning of July 24, the lovely **Hanagasa Junkō** (Flower Umbrella procession) also takes place. If you'd like to see a *geiko-san* (the Kyoto word for *geisha*), this is your chance.

Prioritizing what to enjoy may be one of the greatest Gion Festival challenges. Consult the **Exploration** section if you'd like an overview of activities, or the **Schedule** if you'd like to plan by dates of your visit.

Geiko-san await the beginning of the Hanagasa Junkō.

Gion Festival's Global Relevance Today

Presented annually by thousands of volunteers, the Gion Festival is a fascinating self-organizing institution. With more than a millennium of rich history, the Gion Festival offers an excellent case study for sustainability and community resilience. Given that it has continued annually for so many centuries, what can this teach us? What is it about the Gion Festival that has made it so meaningful to so many people for so many generations? What continues to make it worthy of our interest and support today?

As the human population grows and the planet feels smaller, these are increasingly important questions. The answers are even more critical. As we explore the Gion Festival, see how much of it functions *well*, and how it ceaselessly adapts. This empowers the festival to confidently stride each year into the future.

As we learn to pursue ecological, social, and financial sustainability together—for our own benefit and that of the global community—cultural sustainability can bring a richness of experience to the other three. Importantly, what positive roles can tourism play in this?

Up until the late 20th century, though the Gion Festival was renowned across Japan, it was still primarily run by and for the local community and Kyoto. Nowadays festival go-ers include people from all over the country, and around the world. Though it offers many activities and experiences, the festival was never designed for "things to do." People paid respects to deities at Yasaka Shrine and at floats, passed time eating and drinking with friends, and enjoyed the sights. This continues to be a good approach. And this book shares with you all the other amazing things you may like to experience.

A neighborhood celebration welcoming more than a million visitors.

A Japanese proverb, *Ichigo, ichi-e,* translates roughly to: "This special moment, this unique coming together." It celebrates the extraordinariness of each moment, and how quickly the moment is gone forever. This kind of relaxed appreciation is still at the heart of the Gion Festival. Enjoy.

BRIEF HISTORY OF THE GION FESTIVAL

Considered one of the oldest urban festivals in the world, the Gion Festival is a tradition rooted in the culture of the ancient imperial capital of Kyoto, founded in the year 794 C.E. The Gion Festival is a giant collection of purification rituals and prayers to prevent death, illness and the suffering they bring. At the same time, it is a celebration of the fleeting beauty of this life. You could say it's all about impermanence.

Deeply rooted in Japan's rainy season, the Gion Festival sometimes takes place amidst typhoons.

Midsummer Kyoto in the year 869 C.E. was like today: unbearably hot and humid, and subject to heavy storms. This is the rainy season in the subtropics.

But in 869, Kyotoites were suffering from a terrible epidemic. It is said that the Kamo River had overflowed, and later was filled with corpses. Surely, the Japanese Emperor Seiwa believed, some vengeful spirits were punishing the people for an unknown wrongdoing. Hoping for relief, he sponsored a ritual to pacify the deities.

GORYŌ-E: MAKING PEACE WITH ANGRY SPIRITS

In that earlier age, people believed that any misfortune was caused by *onryō*, or angry spiritual entities. By making offerings to such deities—which could include anything that might please them, such as respect, beauty, entertainment, good deeds, etc.—they could be transformed into benevolent spirits called *goryō*. It was believed that *onryō* could cause a lot of problems in one's life, but *goryō* were powerful and helpful allies.[5]

Emperor Seiwa's ritual was called a *goryō-e,* a meeting with benevolent deities, to try to ensure peace. He called for 66 *hoko*—like a spear, carried upright—to pay respects to the gods. Each hoko represented a region of the country at that time, to ensure the entire nation was purified and protected from harm. It took place at a garden pond named Shinsen-en, in the southern part of the Imperial Palace grounds.[6]

---

[5] This is nearly identical to beliefs I encountered studying syncretic shamanic traditions in the Brazilian Amazon. There, people believed that our own attempts to live a virtuous life could inspire troublesome spirits to voluntarily convert into beneficial ones.

[6] Amazingly, the Shinsen-en garden and pond are still there, and appropriately otherworldly. Located at the Oike-Ōmiya

THE GION FESTIVAL

We can guess that the *goryō-e* ritual helped, because the next time pestilence struck, the emperor called for another one. And another one. And so on. After a century, the rituals became an annual event. By the year 1000 C.E. the *hoko* had morphed into floats with wheels, many still possessing a spear- (*hoko-*) like feature at the top of the float, as they do today.

Early history about the Gion Festival is not well known outside specialized academic circles. We do know that, as time passed, the *hoko* began to include banners and umbrellas. Additionally, they were accompanied by music and dance, considered additional means of communication with the spiritual realm. We can see these historic forms today with **Ayagasa Boko** and **Shijō Kasa Boko**.

Shijō Kasa Boko's float includes an umbrella float (back left) accompanied by musicians and dancing boys.

There is also some evidence of **women**'s participation in the Gion Festival's early history, though it is relatively scarce and generally played down. We also know that women enjoyed status as shamanesses in Shintō rituals

---

intersection, it is still part of the route of the Gion Festival's **kankōsai** procession on July 24. One festival patron who's 100 years old at the time of writing told me that everyone still called the Gion Festival the "Gion Goryō-e" when he was a boy.

in the past. Japanese has a word for "shamaness"—*miko*—but not for "shaman."

When Did the Gion Festival Take Its Modern Form?

The spears and umbrellas on wheels continued to morph into more complex and decorated floats, still called *hoko* today. Others came to be used as small stages to act out traditional noh theater plays, another way to commune with spirits. These stage-like floats are called *yama*. The two float types are collectively called **yamaboko**. It's believed that the yamaboko floats procession we know today began in the 14th century.

Tokusa Yama shows a scene from a noh play by the genius playwright Zeami.

We also know that, since the Gion Festival became an annual event in 970 C.E., it has only ceased entirely once, for 33 years, due to the civil Ōnin War (1467-77). This war devastated Kyoto. But it also ended the aristocratic and shogunal dominance of Kyoto society, bringing in an unprecedented era of social mobility. When the Gion Festival was relaunched in 1496, the emerging merchant class took the lead. This shaped much of the Gion Festival's unique character: it's

THE GION FESTIVAL

considered one of the world's oldest urban festivals, put on entirely by citizens.

From then on, much of Kyoto's new worldly culture was shaped, and funded, by its wealthy kimono merchants. Downtown Kyoto—around the intersection of Shijō and Muromachi streets—was and is the center of the kimono industry. The Muromachi era was a Golden Age for arts and culture in Kyoto. And Muromachi and Shijō streets are still home to numerous Gion Festival yamaboko floats.

Although the kimono tradespeople were rich, Japan's social hierarchy kept merchants at the bottom. Moreover, since military leaders and aristocrats did not want to be outclassed, laws strictly limited merchants' demonstrations of wealth.

Kimono and the Gion Festival have a long shared history.
Byōbu Matsuri, Shinmachi street.

The Gion Festival provided an optimal loophole. Each Gion Festival *yamaboko* float presented an opportunity for Kyoto's kimono merchants to show off their worldly success and cultural sophistication, while still playing within the rules.

Kyoto was the easternmost destination on the Silk Road, and international connections meant *power*. The Gion Festival community used their floats to advertise that they had overseas contacts, even if only indirectly. After the Tokugawa Shogun virtually closed the entire country to non-Japanese influence in the 1630s, new Gion Festival treasures from abroad—most notably the international **textiles** hung on the floats—were fundamentally black-market goods. The kimono merchants used the floats to flash their prosperity and mock the upper social classes and their regulations, while somehow managing to stay out of trouble.

*Some non-Japanese **textiles** like this 16th-century Belgian tapestry at **Koi Yama** entered Japan after foreign goods were prohibited. Some—like this one—had fascinating journeys to arrive in the Gion Festival.*

Apparently, it was around this same time, at the outset of the Edo Period (1603-1868), that **women** ceased to participate in the Gion Festival.[7] The Tokugawa shogunate was strongly influenced by a revival of ancient Confucian values from China, which helped lay the ground for political stability and economic growth. The Tokugawa shogunate also interpreted neo-Confucianism to socially and legally establish men squarely above women. This greatly

---

[7] Change happens: a small number of young **women** have participated in the "traditionally all-male" festival since the end of the 20th century.

restricted women's freedom. It also placed a major burden on men's shoulders, probably sowing seeds for the modern phenomenon of *karōshi*, death by overwork.

Kyoto culture is famous for its subtlety. Yet the occasion to show off became an integral part of the Gion Festival culture, bequeathing us the incredible floats and magnificent treasures we enjoy viewing today. Consequently, the Gion Festival has been renowned across the country for centuries: people longed to see it in their lifetime. And each Gion Festival neighborhood rivalled one another to have the most sumptuous and internationally decorated *yamaboko* float. Even until the late 1900s, each Gion Festival **community** kept its activities secret to enhance their competitive edge.

People who dreamed of one day seeing the Gion Festival in person would have bought woodblock prints like this 19th-century triptych by Utagawa Sadahide. The Gion Festival may be among the oldest brands on the planet.

But it's not all about flamboyant displays. Another aspect of the history of the Gion Festival ***yamaboko***

floats is told in tales of fire. Most of the floats have been destroyed several times by great fires that consumed Kyoto, vulnerably built of wood and paper. This is one reason the ***chōnai*** neighborhoods are so proud of their floats and treasures: they are incredible survivors. They've been rebuilt from nothing, by people who had lost everything, time and again over hundreds of years. The centuries-old treasures we enjoy are still here because they were heroically saved from major fires by local people who risked their lives to preserve them for posterity.

What About the Gion Festival Today?

Reflecting this history, the Gion Festival persists as a symbol of communities' ability to rise above hardship. Besides the major fires that devastated the Gion Festival floats and neighborhoods, illnesses and deaths related to summer rains continued into the mid-1900s. Many Gion Festival patrons never returned from World War II.

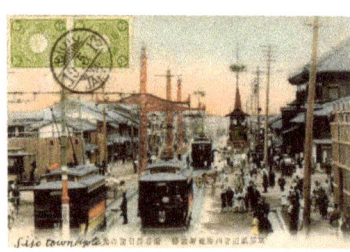

A postcard of Gion Festival floats with streetcars on Shijō street, circa 1940.

For six years, starting in 1945, U.S. occupying forces banned public gatherings, including the Gion Festival procession. For those years the festival was reduced to just a few floats being built, and being pulled a few blocks and back.

Postwar tax reform meant that private individuals kept fewer profits, which scaled down the Gion Festival's culture of wealth. Religion and government were also separated by law. This presented challenges for the government to financially support this spiritual festival. It also led to the festival becoming more material and less spiritual. Postwar poverty forced people in the tightly-knit Gion Festival communities to sell their properties, including some of their historic festival **kaisho** meeting places. Other rapid postwar changes included **women** being allowed to board **yamaboko floats** for the first time in centuries.

The Gion Festival had always included two parts: the **Saki Matsuri** and **Ato Matsuri**. The Saki Matsuri welcomes the **Yasaka Shrine deities** to downtown Kyoto, and the Ato Matsuri escorts them back, thanking them and bidding them farewell for another year. However, by the early 1960s, traffic, crowds, and tourism interests sparked their amalgamation into one intensive week-long celebration, July 10-17. For nearly half a century, there was just one floats' procession on July 17, while the Yasaka Shrine deities still came and went in their **mikoshi** during the **shinkōsai** and **kankōsai** on July 17 and 24.

This disturbed traditionalists. How could the Yasaka Shrine deities come and go, with a welcoming floats' procession but no farewell procession? To them, it didn't make sense.

Meanwhile, Japan's economic bubble led to climbing real estate values in the late 20th century. Many historic families in Gion Festival neighborhoods could not afford inheritance taxes on their traditional homes.

Demolishing them and building apartments, office buildings, parking lots, and hotels became a profitable alternative. As a result, the number of people who live and work in the area year-round has greatly decreased. This means that the number of people who have the knowhow and ability to make the Gion Festival happen has also declined.

Downtown oasis: Traditional buildings in the Gion Festival neighborhoods have interior gardens like this.

Girls began playing **festival music** on some floats in the 1990s. Around the same time, a landmark survey of non-Japanese **textiles** in the Gion Festival revealed the high international value of its unique collection. Japan's economic bubble burst, and the kimono industry—the longtime backbone of the Gion Festival—collapsed. Gion Festival neighborhood associations continue to adapt their legal and financial structures, so that, for example, donations could be tax-deductible.

Ironically, the enormous crowds attending the Gion Festival and accompanying logistical challenges formed part of the rationale to separate the two parts of the festival once more. To the delight of traditionalists who continue to honor the festival's spiritual meaning, the Gion Festival returned to its original format in 2014, with two float processions on July 17 and 24.

The Gion Festival has survived all of these ups and downs, for more than 1150 years. It's an unsurpassed symbol of sustainability and the enduring human spirit.

Nowadays, like everywhere, suffering in Kyoto has taken new forms. Instead of "summer sickness," nuclear fallout, climate change, and global pandemics make our common future uncertain.

The collapse of Japan's economic bubble, the implosion of the kimono industry, deterioration of the social and cultural fabric in Kyoto's urban core, and evolving gender roles are all challenging the traditional identity of the Gion Festival.

Ritual offerings of rice, salt, sake, and a purifying leaf. **Koi Yama**.

Nonetheless, each year the Gion Festival continues as a giant prayer for the wellbeing of Kyoto, its people, and visitors. It also serves as a celebration of what's known in Japanese as *mono-no-aware,* the breathtaking, fleeting beauty of this world.

GION FESTIVAL'S SPIRITUAL ROOTS

Yasaka Shrine: The God of Storms and Goddess of Rice

Pre-existing the ancient capital of Kyoto (founded in 794), the Yasaka Shrine's origins date to 656. At that time, one legend holds, a representative from the Silla Kingdom (modern-day Korean peninsula) brought the worship of the deity Susano-o-no-Mikoto from Ox-Head Mountain in Silla.

Though now Shintō, Japan's native animistic tradition, Yasaka Shrine was also Buddhist at its origins and for most of its history. Its original name was *Gion-sha*, meaning "Jeta Grove Shrine." If called a shrine in Japan, it is Shintō, while a temple is Buddhist. Jeta Grove was the Buddha's first monastery in India. The creation of a Gion Shrine shows how adaptable Japanese spirituality can be, by naming a Shintō shrine after a Buddhist temple.

Susano-o-no-Mikoto is still revered as Yasaka Shrine's central deity. He's the Shintō god of storms, and the tempestuous younger brother of Amaterasu, Japan's sun goddess. It was believed that epidemics are carried on the winds of storms, and Susano-o has the power to bring storms and plague, or protect us from them. Since Kyoto's "summer sickness" was also linked to downpours and resulting floods, we can understand how praying to the god of storms felt important.

Susano-o-no-Mikoto slaying an eight-headed dragon to rescue Kushi Inada Hime, 19th-century woodblock print by Toyohara Chikanobu.

The *Kojiki* and the *Nihongi*, the two oldest books of Japanese history, describe the epic adventure of how Susano-o cleverly and bravely rescued Princess Kushi-Inada, the Japanese goddess of rice, from a deadly eight-headed dragon.[8] Kushi-Inada is the second resident deity at Yasaka Shrine. Because Susano-o saved Kushi-Inada, and because life-giving rice thrives thanks to the freshwater coming in with summer storms, Susano-o is also recognized as a god of love. Susano-o and Kushi-Inada's eight children, as a group,

---

[8] Basil Hall Chamberlain, *The Kojiki* (Boston: Tuttle, 1981) pp. 72-76. W.G. Aston, *Nihongi* (Boston: Tuttle, 1972) pp 52-58.

are considered Yasaka Shrine's third deity. While the Gion Festival was designed as a ritual to prevent illness and death, that theme is coupled with this aspect of promoting life. The floats bring fertility to city streets, with their *hoko* masts as ancient symbols of phallic potency.

What about Princess Kushi-Inada? Females enjoyed more prominence in ancient Japan compared to later in history. For example, there were six female emperors in the 6th-8th centuries, but only two since then.[9] Given the importance of rice in Japanese culture, it seems likely that reverence for Kushi-Inada may have been stronger in antiquity than it is now.

Chimaki

Chimaki talismans are hung outside the door to keep epidemics away. Written on them are the float name and "Connected to Somin Shōrai."

Another Gion-related legend describes how a poor man named Somin Shōrai provided hospitality when Susano-o-no-Mikoto needed a place to stay the night. Wealthier homes had turned him away. Susano-o rewarded Somin by

---

[9] The last Japanese empress ruled in the late 1700s. Currently, Japanese law dictates that only men can reign, a dilemma since the current emperor has one child, a daughter. Public opinion favors changing the laws to allow an empress to reign.

teaching him that hanging talismanic straw at his door would protect him and his family from epidemics. The omnipresent *chimaki* charms on sale[10] at nearly every float are part of this tradition, as are the large straw hoops we can walk through at Yasaka Shrine and some floats.[11] Chimaki are also an important source of revenue to support ongoing conservation of the festival floats.

The Ox-Headed Emperor

In addition to Susano-o-no-Mikoto, an important Gion Festival deity is the protector against epidemics, the Buddhist-derived *Gozu Tennō*, meaning "ox-headed emperor." We can see calligraphy scrolls invoking his name at central locations in many **yamaboko floats**' treasure areas.

Gozu Tennō was originally Gośīrṣa, a protector deity from the Buddha's first monastery in India, Jeta

Ritual offerings below a scroll with the calligraphy, "Gion Ox-Headed Emperor," at **Yamabushi Yama**.

---

[10] If you'd like to take chimaki overseas, declare them as an agricultural product in customs and put them in your freezer for three full days as soon as you get home. This prevents the spread of potentially harmful organisms.

[11] At Yasaka Shrine on July 31 (see **Schedule**) and at **Yamabushi Yama** and **En-no-Gyōja Yama**.

Grove, which translates in Japanese to *Gion Shōja*. This became another name for Yasaka Shrine, and Gion also became the name of the surrounding district. Gozu Tennō is sometimes known as a god of plagues, though a protector against plagues is more likely since he's also considered a manifestation of Medicine Buddha.

In Mahayana Buddhism, Gozu Tennō has a counterpart in the ox-headed Yamantaka, a fierce protector against death. Up until the mid-20th century, deaths in Kyoto from "summer sickness" were not uncommon, so we can understand why Gozu Tennō/Yamantaka became important for the Gion Festival.

A rare painting of Gozu Tennō, **Hashi Benkei Yama** *collection.*

Gion/Yasaka Shrine has always been nationally prominent, and today boasts more than 3,000 sub-shrines across the country. The original ***goryō-e*** **ritual** to placate angry spirits eventually conjoined with prayers to these two renowned protectors from epidemics residing at the illustrious Gion Shrine, and it became the "Gion Goryō-e." It was still called this as recently as the early 1900s, according to festival elders. Since then, it gradually gained its current name, the Gion Festival.

Here Be Dragons

Yasaka Shrine shimmers with still more mysteries and myths. Kyoto was modeled after Xi'an, then the capital of China, and similarly located and developed according to feng shui, or geomancy. According to that system, a different protector animal resides in each of the four directions. In the east is a blue dragon.[12] Yasaka Shrine's main hall or *honden* is built over a pond deep in the earth, and it's said that the blue dragon lives there.[13]

In addition, dragons relate to the element of water, central to Kyoto's summer rainy season and related illnesses. This is why there are so many dragons—especially blue ones—decorating the various Gion Festival floats.

In 1868, Shintō was embraced by the Meiji government as the national religion. As a result, all "Buddhist shrines" had the Buddhist part separated out by government order. Susano-o-no-Mikoto and Gozu Tennō,

A blue dragon textile, **En-no-Gyōja Yama**, *points to the directional protector residing at Yasaka Shrine. China, late 17th century.*

---

[12] A scarlet sparrow lives in the south, a white tiger in the west, and a black tortoise in the north.

[13] See my YouTube channel, The Gion Festival, for a video on this topic.

considered different manifestations of the same deity until then, were also separated. Gion Shrine became Yasaka Shrine, and officially all Shintō, as did the Gion Festival.

***Naginata Boko's* chigo** *child after a ritual at Yasaka Shrine on July 13.*

Most of the buildings we see at Yasaka Shrine today date to 1654, and it adjoins a beautiful strolling park to the east and temple-rich neighborhoods both to the north and south. You could easily enjoy several hours sightseeing in this area.

Yasaka Shrine flourishes with Gion Festival-related activities throughout the month of July. The shrine sincerely perseveres in undertaking Gion Festival events as Shintō rituals, rather than tourist events. As a result, little information (like schedules or descriptions) is made public, particularly not in English. While this can feel frustrating at times to visitors, it can be rewarding to witness an authentic ritual at a functioning Shintō shrine that's clearly at the center of an active community.

The Shinkōsai Procession

The three Yasaka Shrine deities—Susano-o, Kushi-Inada, and their group of eight children—reside year-round at Yasaka Shrine, except when they

THE GION FESTIVAL

are transported in the three portable *mikoshi* shrines through central Kyoto during the Gion Festival. This important week of travel is meant to purify many different neighborhoods between the shrine and their *otabisho* visiting place at the Shijō-Teramachi intersection, on the nights of July 17 (***shinkōsai***) and 24 (***kankōsai***).

The Kuze koma-gata chigo *at Yasaka Shrine, starting the shinkōsai.*

Chigo, Remnants of Child Mediums

The shinkōsai and kankōsai start and end with formal ceremonies at Yasaka Shrine, some of which include Yasaka Jinja's two "*koma-gata **chigo***," from the district of Kuze. "Chigo" means "immature child." These boys and rituals are the modern remnants of when children were considered pure vessels to receive the spirits of the gods. In ancient times, this was likely a form of shamanic mediumship. Until the late 1800s, every hoko had a chigo-san; today only **Naginata Boko**, **Ayagasa Boko**, and Yasaka Shrine do. Chigo are one of the more eye-catching features of the festival.

Who's Who in the Portable *Mikoshi* Shrines

At the center of the shinkōsai and kankōsai are the three Yasaka Shrine deities in their beautiful portable mikoshi shrines. A unique guild, or *shinyokai,* sponsors each mikoshi. It's a tremendous honor and source of pride to undertake this responsibility and tradition each year. Below are the names of the mikoshi, and who's inside which one. You'll see the respective Japanese characters on the mikoshi themselves and on the *haori* jackets the men wear.

The portable mikoshi *shrines on Yasaka Shrine's traditional* maidono *stage, awaiting their journey downtown. Here Susano-o is in the middle, Princess Kushi Inada is on the left and their children are on the right.*

1) Sanwaka / 三若, also known as 中御座 (naka go-za), is the mikoshi for Susano-o-no-Mikoto. It's six-sided and topped with a phoenix that holds a rice plant in its beak. It also weighs up to 2.5 tons. About 50 men called *yochō* shoulder the weight at any given time, meaning

they are carrying 40kg each. This is a serious commitment, and you can see how focused the yochō are. About 700 men take turns carrying all three mikoshi.[14]

2) Shiwaka / 四若, also known as 東御座 (higashi go-za), is the mikoshi for Princess Kushi Inada. It is four-sided and topped with a round jewel. During the shinkōsai, this one also comes with a mini *higashi-waka-go-za* (東若御座) mikoshi, made especially for the children of guild families.

3) Nishiki / 錦, also known as 西御座 (nishi go-za), contains the deities of the eight children of Susano-o and Kushi-Inada. It's eight-sided, topped with a phoenix, and weighs about two tons. This mikoshi belongs to the famous Nishiki covered food market nearby, and has historic connections with the *bushido* samurai code.

The Kankōsai Procession

Translating to "the return festival," the kankōsai takes place on the evening of July 24. The shinyokai guilds carry the three Gion deities in their mikoshi through different downtown neighborhoods than the shinkōsai, on their way back to Yasaka Shrine. Some go by Shinsen-en pond near the Oike-Ōmiya

---

[14] Thanks to **enjoykyoto.net** (see Issue 5) for their excellent descriptions of mikoshi culture.

intersection, the original site of the *goryō-e* ritual that birthed the Gion Festival in the year 869. Learn more about the **kankōsai** in the **Visiting the Gion Festival** section.

The Performing Arts

As we can see from the traditional stages at the heart of Yasaka Shrine, the arts have been an important part of Shintō rituals since time immemorial. As in most (if not all) ancient cultures, Japanese music, dance, and theater were considered a means for human performers to connect with spirits or deities for the benefit of the community.

Of course, the Japanese arts have become less spiritual, along with much of world culture. The Gion Festival gives us an opportunity to see whether we can get a feeling for when the performing arts were more directly connected with communicating with the unseen world. This is still a strong tradition in noh theater, but unfortunately, noh's presence in the Gion Festival

*Girls dancing traditional nihon buyō dance at Yasaka Shrine after the **Hanagasa Junkō** procession on July 24.*

has declined. See the **Dance and Music** or **Schedule** sections for details on dance and music you can enjoy on Yasaka Shrine's two central stages, and elsewhere.

PLEASING THE GODS

Despite the illness, death, and angry spirits, Japanese purification rituals aren't necessarily solemn events. The Japanese word for festival, *matsuri*, means "celebration." According to Shintō, there are spirits and deities—called *kami*—everywhere, in everything. They reside in nature, they get adopted from other cultures, and some people may also become *kami* after death. Like humans, Japanese *kami* have many different personalities: some make merry, get angry, or make mischief—except that kami also have supernatural powers, and do things like cause or guard against floods, epidemics, and other illnesses.

Therefore, people believed that it was in our best self-interest to please the gods. We humans may try to please kami both by acting virtuously—living a good life and making offerings to the deities, for example—and by celebrating! Traditionally, playing music, dancing, acting bravely, having sex,

A Shintō priest performs a purification ritual to prepare **Ayagasa Boko** *float for the festival.*

drinking sake, and paying respects at shrines are all considered pleasing to Shintō kami.

And Still More Gods

We've noted that the Gion Festival is spiritually very well endowed. Besides the deities residing at Yasaka Shrine, each Gion Festival **yamaboko float** also has its own deities that it pays respects to. Each one comes with fascinating myths and legends, all of which shape the character of the community. What's more, each float undertakes numerous rituals for its own deity, float, and community each year. Learn more on each of the **yamaboko floats**' pages.

Ascetic yamabushi *monks and nuns chant the Heart Sutra to pay respects at* ***Yamabushi Yama***.

COMMUNITY: THE GION FESTIVAL *CHŌNAI*

The Gion Festival exists thanks to a unique coming together of interdependent, semi-autonomous neighborhood associations, called *chōnai*. The chōnai are essential: each one builds, operates, and maintains its own **yamaboko float** and its **treasures**. The festival's 1150-plus years of illustrious history represent a triumph of community collaboration difficult to match anywhere on the planet.

Traditionally the Gion Festival and floats' treasure areas were a time and place for community members to enjoy coming together, like here at **Ashikari Yama**.

Each geographic chōnai consists of a diamond shape, with a north-south street down the middle. Historically, Gion Festival chōnai members were families and businesses, who often lived and worked in the same building. They were joined by their employees, who also lived and/or worked in the neighborhood.

Having a place in these Gion Festival neighborhoods was a coveted privilege: prospective residents had to apply to the chōnai, meet rigorous requirements, and earn responsibility. Sometimes the communities were gated. In case of poor behavior or economic weakness, people and businesses were required to leave. Historically, when something was needed for the festival, Gion Festival chōnai residents and employees jumped to get it done. Then and even now, many businesses slowed or even ceased operations during much of the month-long festival.

The beginning of a lifetime of commitment with **Urade Yama**.

"I work very hard all year, so I can take July off to work for the Gion Festival," laughed a kimono company president who is in leadership roles at one float during the **Saki Matsuri**, and at another during the **Ato Matsuri**.

All this has greatly changed. Nowadays most chōnai residents work outside the chōnai or even outside of Kyoto. Most employers and colleagues (both within and outside the chōnai) don't feel an urgent need to grant chōnai residents or workers time off to support the Gion Festival. While different chōnai are experimenting with new arrangements (see below), an effective new model has yet to fill this growing gap in the Gion Festival's supportive structure. So what the chōnai do today, and how they manage to do it, are all the more impressive.

Each chōnai has its own personality. Some are very family-oriented; others emphasize the "celebration" side. Some orient around a historic home, family, or business. Some focus on preserving traditions, and others are interested in creatively adapting to changing times.

Family time at **Hakurakuten Yama**.

What happens with the float has always been decided collectively[15] by the chōnai members. In addition, the character and interests of individual chōnai members can greatly shift the character of a chōnai. A history, art, or calligraphy buff, for example, might document the float's treasures or translate its archaic archives into modern Japanese, increasing everyone's understanding. In such ways, new discoveries are regularly revealed about the floats, their history, and

---

[15] Since democracy has become common in our modern era this seems natural, but it's remarkable given the aristocratic and feudal nature of most of Japanese history.

treasures. When the resources are available, it's an exciting frontier.

This convenience store in the Gion Festival floats' neighborhood wins kudos for maintaining a traditional facade.

The rise and fall of the Gion Festival yamaboko and their treasures have always mirrored the fluctuations in fortunes of its chōnai residents. Before Japan's economic bubble burst in the 1990s, this part of Kyoto bustled with prosperous kimono-related businesses: silk dealers, wholesalers, dyers, and the like. Climbing real estate values and the post-bubble collapse of the kimono industry have transformed the Gion Festival chōnai. Historic homes and companies have given way to apartment buildings,

*Chōnai members restored **Shijō Kasa Boko** with its children dancers to the **Saki Matsuri** procession in 1985 after an absence of over a century.*

seasonal residents, hotels, office buildings, hourly parking lots, restaurants, and convenience stores.

Ironically, apartments and hotels appeal to out-of-town owners and visitors who are attracted to the Gion Festival environment. But these people often have no clear channels to effectively support the future of the festival they've come to experience. The rapidly maturing age and decreasing size of a constantly present population introduces a considerable set of challenges to the Gion Festival, perhaps new in its long history. It also highlights what amazing things a relatively small population of elders can achieve.

Because few young people connected to the Gion Festival live and work in the area today, ready inheritors of the elders' knowledge and experience are also small in number. New residents and businesses who have recently arrived from elsewhere are busy with their own lives and work, and often don't have the awareness, inclination, or easy ways to meaningfully contribute to the Gion Festival. Even when a new arrival is willing to undertake this significant commitment and privilege, training new people takes time and energy, which are already in short supply.

The power of community: **Hakurakuten Yama** *chōnai members hang their 17th-century Gobelin tapestry.*

Meanwhile, there's a significant socio-cultural gap between historic chōnai residents and new arrivals, one that's challenging to bridge. Traditionally, commitment to the Gion Festival was for a lifetime, often numerous lifetimes, as one generation raised the next within the festival traditions. One festival musician in his 70s told me he'd been participating since he was five years old. Quitting in frustration or due to changing schedules or interests simply never happened.

It's clear that new kinds of increased participation are needed, and will benefit everyone who attends the Gion Festival. Besides ensuring its healthy future, some floats have treasures and archives that have rarely come out of storage within memory, simply because of limited human power. The festival floats are nicknamed "Moving Museums," but no museum catalog exists. Research possibilities are logistically very challenging.

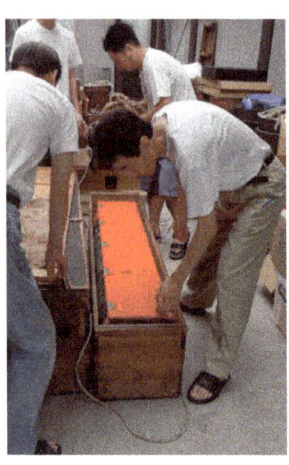

*Setting up **Abura Tenjin Yama**. Chōnai members build, decorate, design, commission, host, disassemble, organize, conserve, repair, and do paperwork for the float, community, and its treasures. And have families and day jobs.*

There's also been major growth in non-chōnai support of the Gion Festival since the late 20th century. With World Heritage status, Japanese Important Cultural Property status, tourism revenue, government subsidies, and the like, the Gion Festival's foundation is morphing. And yet the festival know-how remains in the hands, hearts, and minds of the relatively small—and currently elderly—number of residents in the *chōnai* communities.

Government financial support is welcome and needed. The chōnai has always given the best available to the Gion Festival, and conserving, restoring, and replacing the best—exposed each year to Kyoto's rainy season—is costly and time-consuming.[16] The associated paperwork and organization take time and skill.

Many journalists, academics, students, authors, etc. would like time with these elders so that we can learn more about the festival. And these elders undertake it all good-naturedly.

In short, more than ever, these festival patrons remain steadfast champions of the Gion Festival traditions.

Stepping into the Challenge

We all face our own version of contemporary challenges: how can we respond *well* to the extremely rapid pace of modern change? This is one of the pressing questions of our times. And some *chōnai* are creating innovative ways to rise to this occasion. We can celebrate the power of community by noting some of the Gion Festival chōnai's successes:

- **Ayagasa Boko** drew on extensive historical and anthropological research to relaunch its float in 1979. Today it partners with Kyoto's Buddhist University so that graduate students may include participating in the Gion Festival as part of their fieldwork.

---

[16] Replacing a set of four wooden wheels for a hoko float cost ¥20 million yen or about US$164,000 in 2007. Making a replica of one antique textile can cost around US$150,000 and take two years to complete.

- While **Kita Kannon Yama** has resolutely conserved the festival's best traditional cityscape—called *machinami* in Japanese—**Minami Kannon Yama** has tirelessly grown a new machinami on Shinmachi street, with a mix of conservation, restoration, and quality replica facades.

*Hōka Boko's hikizome in the **Minami Kannon Yama** neighborhood's cultivated cityscape.*

- **Tokusa Yama** was an early award-winning innovator in the modern Gion Festival, inviting corporate sponsors to partner with them by donating transportation and other services.
- As you'll see, understanding the history, meaning, and origins of the floats and their treasures can be a challenge. **Kuronushi Yama** launched live public interpretations at their display area. A knowledgeable chōnai member describes the origins and meaning of their float and treasures in Japanese.

*Interpreting a 16th-century upcycled Chinese woman's robe with a dragon, at **Kuronushi Yama**.*

- After World War II, **Kankō Boko** was the first Gion Festival float to allow women to board in at least 300 years. It also became the first to welcome

THE GION FESTIVAL

female **ohayashi musicians**, in 1993. Besides proclaiming themselves as Gion Festival's "democratic" or egalitarian float, including women potentially doubles the pool of people available for community roles.

- The **Taka Yama** chōnai has committed to the process of reintroducing their float into the Gion Festival in the 2020s, after an absence of nearly 200 years. Their **ohayashi music** troupe performances during the **Ato Matsuri** are complemented by a cool multimedia presentation.

- In an era troubled by social isolation, both **Tōrō Yama** and **Ōfune Boko** have intentionally used the re-introduction of their floats (in 1981 and 2014, respectively) to vitalize their communities. **Tōrō Yama** approaches its participation in the Gion Festival as a form of media, or communication, among chōnai members and with the general public. It also uses the Gion Festival as an opportunity to develop leadership among chōnai members.

- The **Ōfune Boko** chōnai increased their social impact by conserving a traditional **kyōmachiya** townhouse—now its treasure display area—in the community as part of the project. In addition, they created what may be the Gion

*Architectural conservation at **Ōfune Boko**.*

Festival's first crowdfunding campaign, an innovative new way to fund their float's restoration.
- **Hakurakuten Yama** has partnered with an international student program at Doshisha University, resulting in the most-translated (12+ languages) float description of the entire festival.
- After wartime construction[17] and downtown core development left no residents in its chōnai, **Naginata Boko** reworked its participant structure to cultivate one of the festival's most robust musical troupes and memberships.
- **Fune Boko** and **Hachiman Yama** worked with Ritsumeikan University's Arts Research Center to take high-precision measurements and images of their floats, as well as of Fune Boko's treasures. Fune Boko's measurements were adapted to rebuild **Ōfune Boko**, whose construction methods were lost when it burned in 1864's Great Genji Fire.[18] Some of Fune Boko's treasures are now available year-round for research in high-resolution digital imagery.

*Exploring a **Fune Boko** textile digitally via touchscreen at a temporary exhibit.*

---

[17] Their and some other floats' locations, on the north side of Shijō street, were demolished to make an anti-bombing firebreak.

[18] This historic fire started with the Hamaguri Gate rebellion, a protest against the weakening Tokugawa shogunate. The fire spread, destroying much of Kyoto.

THE GION FESTIVAL

- By 1995 **Koi Yama**'s chōnai residents had shrunk to just 21, with a large apartment building's construction planned. The chōnai developed a successful, socially innovative scheme to invite the 250-plus new apartment dwellers to participate meaningfully in the Gion Festival, in a mutually supportive relationship with chōnai natives.

Who is in the Gion Festival Community?

Strictly speaking, only chōnai residents or employees are a part of the festival. However, their family, friends, employees from elsewhere, and colleagues may be invited to participate too. Though I'm not a chōnai resident, I consider myself part of the community. As mentioned, I consider the million-plus visitors part of the community too.

*The **Kita Kannon Yama** neighborhood, one of the most traditional.*

And what do community members do? We support one another.

It may be only for an hour, an evening, or a day. But while we're at the festival, we can show some appreciation for the Gion Festival *chōnai* and other community members. It could be a thank you, a smile, or buying a souvenir at a favorite float to fund their conservation efforts. After all, these people graciously provide their resources as a service to keep the Gion Festival going for us to enjoy. And our appreciation fuels their efforts.

Women in the Gion Festival

The ongoing dialogue about women's participation became topical in the early 1990s, when a folding screen—dating to around 1615, before the **Tokugawa/ Edo Era**—surfaced, depicting women playing music on a Gion Festival float. Was it a historical representation? Or an imaginary one? Remember, cross-dressing has a long history in Japan, particularly in the arts like kabuki and noh theater.

The late medieval historian Professor Haruko Wakita strongly argued that ancient manuscripts in Yasaka Shrine's archives document women's participation in past Gion Festivals. These included Shintō shamanesses and women dancers on the floats in the Middle Ages, she maintained.

Organization of the Gion Festival floats' chōnai is such that each one has some autonomy about what they choose to do or not. In 2001, the Gion Festival Floats Federation, a loose organizing body, decreed that women could participate in the festival. This was no doubt in part because some were already participating in at least two floats' musical troupes. No other floats have publicly followed this trend,[19]

---

[19] There may be more women participating that I'm unaware of: discretion is a Kyoto virtue.

but at another float, women carpenters help build it, and women's roles and responsibilities are increasing in general.

Kankō Boko, in particular, has been an outspoken supporter of women's participation and has welcomed girls and women in their **ohayashi music** troupe and in other important roles.[20] There are female musicians at **Minami Kannon Yama** as well. "It happened naturally," the father of one of the female musicians at Minami Kannon Yama explained to me. "She heard the music all the time as a girl, liked it, and wanted to play. We asked, and everyone said 'okay.'"

*The all-female Heisei Onna Boko ohayashi playing during the **kankōsai**.*

Kankō Boko also very publicly supports an independent women's float, called *Heisei Onna Boko,* which translates roughly to "Contemporary Women's Float."[21] It is dedicated to **Princess Kushi-Inada**, goddess of rice and Gion Festival/Yasaka Shrine deity. This community of women and supporters have built

---

[20] I asked the former director of Kankō Boko's float association why they were so open to women participating in the Gion Festival. He replied that he read Prof. Wakita's book and believed her arguments to be true.

[21] *Heisei* was the Imperial Era from 1989-2019.

a float structure, but so far have no sacred statue nor decorations of their own.

About 50 women actively practice, and perform **gionbayashi** music in various festivals a few times a year. On occasion, their float gets constructed to participate in other festival processions, or displayed, or used for performances of their music. I had the unexpected pleasure of hearing them perform in the Gion Festival **kankōsai** in 2019, as a special activity marking the festival's 1150th anniversary.

But the Heisei Onna Boko has never taken part in the floats' portion of the Gion Festival. Since the latter is an officially designated Important Cultural Property and a recognized UNESCO World Heritage event, there are many regulations designed to conserve the existing festival traditions for posterity. Some of these regulations can be interpreted to mean that Heisei Onna Boko can't participate, since that is not a part of the Gion Festival tradition.

There are logistical challenges, as well. Since each float belongs to a chōnai neighborhood, and has for centuries, what to do with a float that has no chōnai neighborhood, like Heisei Onna Boko?

*Helping out at **Yamabushi Yama**. What roles do they aspire to?*

The Onna Boko website[22] argues that the festival shouldn't

---

[22] Onnaboko.com (Japanese only).

be limited to people in the chōnai. And it's true that many festival participants today come from outside the chōnai they support.

As of today, there is no consensus on women riding on Gion Festival floats or walking in their processions. Some men are for women participating, and some women (friends of mine, too) are against it. Some feel it would be too disruptive, while others argue it would bring vitality.

Gender roles in Japan are very different from the developed West, and it takes time to understand how men and women in Japan relate to power dynamics in relationship. Some wives of Gion Festival patrons have never seen the floats processions, and don't mind. In general, they are diminutive, gracious, gentle, and have their own kind of sovereignty and power. I wonder, what kind of roles will today's Japanese girls want to hold when they become women? Again, we come back to the question of how we can respond well to change.

New traditions: Men and women Tōrō Yama chōnai members together in a commemorative photo in 2008.

As mentioned, each *chōnai* and other bodies (such as Yasaka Shrine) answers this question in their own way. Based on my 25-plus years of researching the festival, I can say that women provide enormous support to the festival, although it's largely from behind the scenes. And each year more are participating in more visible roles, and their contributions are more clearly valued.

While the Gion Festival community and interested observers like myself continue to discuss these topics, four females have maintained prominent roles in the Gion Festival for centuries. Kannon, the Buddhist bodhisattva of compassion, is honored at **Minami Kannon Yama** and **Kita Kannon Yama**; Japan's primordial sun goddess, Amaterasu, is celebrated at **Iwatō Yama**; the empress-shamaness Jingū is revered at **Fune Boko**, **Ōfune Boko**, and **Urade Yama**; and the goddess Suzuka is revered at **Suzuka Yama**.

A statue of Izumo no Okuni, on the northwest corner of the Shijō bridge over the Kamo River in the Gion district.

Finally, the Gion Festival also features the comparatively small but very feminine **Hanagasa Junkō** (Flower Umbrella Procession). It's a separate, smaller procession that takes place during the **Ato Matsuri**, on July 24. After participating in the Hanagasa Junkō, dancers and musicians perform for several hours as an offering to the **Yasaka Shrine deities**. Among other presentations, geisha perform a "Kabuki Dance."

THE GION FESTIVAL

Kabuki theater's foundress—and perhaps a Shintō shamaness[23]—was Izumo no Okuni. It's said she performed this same Kabuki Dance in 1603 on the banks of the Kamo River, in the Gion district. Kabuki (in a weird historical twist, now exclusively male) became wildly popular, as Okuni captured the public's attention with her talent and liberal sensibilities. She danced flamboyantly, wearing a sword and men's clothing.

A young dancer shares some of her Sagi Mai *(Heron Dance) for the* Hanagasa Junkō.

The Hanagasa Junkō is appreciated for its beauty, grace, and colorful, enchanting presentation. The same is true for the associated dances and music, mostly performed by geisha and other women and girls. It seems these performances hold more meaning than we currently appreciate.

---

[23] Okuni was a *miko* at a Shintō shrine. Interestingly the Japanese word *miko* is translated as both "shamaness" and the less formidable "shrine maiden." Some histories refer to her as a "temple dancer" or prostitute. Descriptions of the role of miko are similarly varied and unclear. Hopefully someday soon we'll understand more about this remarkable woman.

ART TREASURES

Legend holds that eighth-century painter Wu Daozi (Jap.: Godōshi) painted a dragon so lifelike that it flew off the page. Japanese embroidery based on a painting by Ishida Yūtei (teacher of Maruyama Ōkyo), 1785, **Kakkyō Yama**.

Reportedly, the Buddha said that the path to enlightenment is in the details. The path to enjoying the Gion Festival is, too. Its decorative elements represent the uncountable fruits of contemplative absorption and international wisdom traditions channeled through the arts and ritual. These can help us enjoy some blissful delight.

THE GION FESTIVAL

At times, the festival can feel overwhelming. These are good occasions to absorb yourself in the details of its artistic treasures. For centuries, Japanese have cultivated the arts—aikidō, sadō (tea ceremony), kadō (ikebana), shodō (calligraphy)—as spiritual paths to increase bliss, clarity, and wisdom for the benefit of all beings. While the craftspeople who created the Gion Festival arts may not have had that as their specific motivation, we can get a sense of the high meditative concentration required to create such exalted works of art. After all, "dō" means "Path of," borrowed from Taoism.

*A metal hook for tassels in the shape of a mantis, **Tōrō Yama**.*

If you take the time to visit the floats' treasure display areas, you'll see priceless treasures up close, enjoy traditional Kyoto **kyōmachiya architecture**, and get a feel for the local **chōnai** community. Written explanations, especially in English, are still somewhat infrequent within the Gion Festival tradition, so feast your eyes and other senses.

*So much beauty: where to look? Ceiling detail, **Tsuki Boko**.*

The vast majority of artistic treasures we see today at the Gion Festival are offerings from the local **chōnai** neighborhood, which each sponsors its own festival **float**. As such they are an exceptional testimony to community-based generosity. This practice continues today, with ongoing chōnai purchases of both antique and newly commissioned works. Whether the works are centuries old or newly made, they represent the best work available in Kyoto, long a world capital for the arts.

As mentioned, the Gion Festival floats as we know them today are products of the kimono industry. Being part of the kimono world calls for weaving and dyeing expertise, as well as vast cultural knowledge: kimono designs tell symbolic stories, revealing the values and interests of the wearer. The Gion Festival floats are similarly rich in spiritual, cultural, and historical allusions.

The ceiling of the Tsuki Boko float, for example, displays gilded paintings of scenes from the world's first novel, *The Tale of Genji*, charmingly depicted within images of folding fans.

At **Tokusa Yama**, carved railing decorations featuring black-lacquer bats flying among gilded clouds refer to the Chinese belief that bats are good luck: the Chinese word for "bat" and "good fortune" sound the same. Numerous floats

Bats of good fortune, railing detail, ***Tokusa Yama****.*

possess textiles with Taoist themes, indicating a historical influence of that philosophy on their communities. Depictions of plants remind us of the seasons, and animals of legends, or perhaps they refer to a larger theme of its particular float.

*Chrysanthemums (and phoenixes) at **Kikusui Boko**, during **hoko tate** construction.*

For example, "kikusui" of the **Kikusui Boko** float, translates to "chrysanthemum water." The float is adorned with chrysanthemums: metal ones, gilded carvings of them, and chrysanthemum designs on their cotton *yukata* kimono. The chrysanthemum water refers to a traditional noh theater drama about gaining eternal life: a 700-year-old boy inscribed Buddhist teachings on chrysanthemum leaves, and then drank the dew on them each morning.

And we see dragons everywhere, particularly blue ones. Firstly these refer to the **dragon** living beneath Yasaka Shrine's main hall. Secondly, dragons relate to water, and thus Kyoto's midsummer rains and the

*Ming dynasty (17th century) dragon textile at **Arare Tenjin Yama**. Many of the Chinese textiles in the Gion Festival are upcycled court robes.*

source of the illnesses that inspired the Gion Festival to begin with.

As we can see throughout the Gion Festival, the **chōnai** commissioned local metalworkers, woodcarvers, and painters to adorn float roofs, railings, posts, and ceilings with mystical, natural, and cultural iconography. Gion Festival commissions also helped Kyoto-based sculptors, weavers, embroiderers, and other artisans to thrive. This longstanding tradition translates to a vast inheritance of centuries of riches from Kyoto's artistic and cultural world.

Phoenix metalwork, roof detail, **Hōka Boko**.

Most of what we see at the Gion Festival today dates to the last four centuries or so, due to repeated great fires that destroyed central Kyoto. New works are also valuable, as they stimulate and showcase the skill of Kyoto's contemporary artisans and their industries. **Tōrō Yama** and **Ayagasa Boko**, for example, recently commissioned new textiles by artists recognized as **Living**

Hashi Benkei Yama's *sacred statue of Benkei was signed and dated by a renowned monk-sculptor in 1693. Real armor, real swords.*

National Treasures. Due to this city's extremely high artistic standards, the best of Kyoto arts have always been of international caliber.

While appreciation of the treasures' value is increasing, you'll see how the Gion Festival was not designed to be a museum. The most knowledgeable people in each float association may be able to tell you how many centuries ago a sacred statue, for example, was carved. Or it may be written down as part of the display, usually in Japanese and dated according to the Imperial calendar system. An exciting frontier of internationally accessible documentation of the Gion Festival's treasures beckons us to explore more deeply.

ARCHITECTURE

Some floats' treasure display areas (also called *kaisho*) are excellent examples of traditional Kyoto **kyōmachiya** townhouses. The generous hospitality built into the **Byōbu Matsuri** allows us to enjoy some interiors of historic families and businesses as well. See the **Explorations** section for details.

TEXTILES

A landmark survey carried out around 1990 by textile experts from American museums, including New York's Metropolitan Museum of Art, confirmed the high value of the Gion Festival's unique international textile collection. The survey established that the diverse tapestries adorning the Gion Festival float exteriors represent a globally unique, rare collection.

Collectively, the textiles span a period of over 700 years, and represent a geographical area from Japan, through China and Persia, to Belgium's 16th-century tapestry workshops. As a collection, the diverse provenance is unique. Some of the textile types exist nowhere else.

An early 17th-century Lahore carpet in excellent condition, **Kankō Boko**.

What heightens the mystique is that, from 1639 to 1853, Japan's trade with the outside world was virtually prohibited. Kyoto kimono merchants' ability to still find ways to import exotic foreign goods dazzled the populace and flashed their power. Most came through the Dutch East India company. They had a trading concession on Kyushu's Dejima Island, and also traded with the indigenous Ainu people—excellent traders—in northernmost Japan. Some European tapestries had more adventurous arrivals, as research commissioned by **Koi Yama** revealed. Many textiles visually depict fascinating tales, from meetings of Taoist sages to the saga of Homer's *Iliad*. Imagine how exotic and evocative these were hundreds of years ago!

Since Kyoto's earliest history it has been the center of Japan's textile production, and pieces made for the Gion Festival were of the highest quality available. So we can say that Japanese textiles in the Gion Festival are among the best ever made in Japan. A comprehensive study of the remarkable Japanese textiles in the Gion Festival is a major milestone still waiting to happen.

Conservators have expressed alarm that these valuable textiles are exposed each year to summer sun and rains. However, some argue that this, too, is a Gion Festival tradition: for centuries textiles have been brought out of storage, hung on the floats, exposed to the elements, aired or dried as much as time allows, and put away. Naturally chōnai members need to get back to their day jobs too. Due to Kyoto's climate and the textiles' type of use, one can be used for about 150 years

Bordered with Kufic script praising Allah, a 13th-14th-century textile of a plum tree branch at **Naginata Boko** *comes from China's Mongol dynasty period. Though very rare worldwide, there are numerous examples of this type of textile in the Gion Festival.*[24]

Intricate Japanese embroidery at **Abura Tenjin Yama**.

---

[24] International textile expert Jeremy Pine argues convincingly that this group of textiles served as military banners carried by Kublai Khan's troops in the 13th-century Mongol attacks on Japan. Pine believes they are woven with animal fur as well as fibers. The Mongols were defeated by typhoons, known as the original *kamikaze* or "winds from the gods." At the time Japanese believed these were sent by the protector god of the Japanese people, Hachiman, celebrated at **Hachiman Yama**.

on average. Anything used longer than that is exceptional, and costly repairs are an ongoing concern.

One modern concession has been plastic rain protection. Additionally, some antique textiles have been recognized by the national government as culturally important. A movement to replace these with replicas has proceeded with enthusiasm, in part thanks to government funding available for this. It's a matter of some debate, because other Kyotoites would prefer to employ contemporary weavers and dyers, and stimulate the festival as well as the contemporary textile industry by commissioning new and original works. No national funding is available for this,[25] but some chōnai find a way to make it happen.

*Not just beautiful and finely woven, this new textile tells the story of a woman who shapeshifts into a dragon, based on an ancient painted scroll. See **Hōka Boko**.*

Each float chooses which textiles to use in the festival, which to conserve or replicate, or whether to commission new ones.[26] Some floats—**Abura Tenjin Yama**, **Ashikari Yama**, and **Taishi Yama**, for example—choose to follow tradition, displaying their

---

[25] There is a workaround, where a chōnai can produce new works if it supports traditional industry. It takes time and a particular skill set to organize this and successfully obtain the funding.

[26] See my YouTube channel, **The Gion Festival**, for a video on "The Great Gion Festival Textile Debate."

THE GION FESTIVAL

ancient textiles throughout the festival as well as commissioning brand new ones instead of replicas. Every commission is customized, because each float's dimensions and needs are unique.

Speaking of textiles, the Gion Festival used to be nicknamed the "Kimono Festival," because people wore the latest fashions showing the finest craftsmanship. Wearing a kimono or yukata today continues this time-honored tradition. If you're a kimono fan, visit **Urade Yama** for the best kimono collection.

This bold indigo design (left) uses a special resist-dyeing technique.

Music

In addition to the displays of the festival's visual treasures from July 12-16 and 21-23, rehearsing *ohayashi* float musicians serenade downtown neighborhoods with their otherworldly *gion-bayashi* music.

To unaccustomed ears, the music may sound disharmonious, or possibly unsettling. It becomes more intriguing when one

Some floats allow visitors on board while the ohayashi musicians play, showing their incredible concentration. **Kankō Boko***, during* **yoiyoiyoiyama***.*

knows that the music has its roots in shamanic ritual. In one sense, the music is designed to please the deities, to win them over as supporters rather than adversaries. Historically, Kyoto's July storms made it a season of illness and death, so the music is also a kind of requiem for the many Gion Festival supporters and Kyotoites who have died.

Ayagasa Boko's ancient-style dance and music will make you want to join in.

Sacred dancers at Shintō shrines performed *kusemai* chant and dance, the predecessor to **noh theater**,[27] to this kind of music. The speeds and rhythms were originally created to bring a shaman/dancer into a trance-like state, similar to Sufi dancing.

We can experience something like this at the Gion Festival today, at the **Ayagasa Boko**. Though ancient screen paintings depict several of the floats with dancers centuries ago, it and **Shijō Kasa Boko** are the only floats to feature them today. Gion Festival floats also used to have people dancing on them, and have had young children, called

---

[27] Kan'ami—the father of Zeami, founder of noh theater as we know it today—learned *kusemai* dance in the mid-14th century from a famous shrine dancer named Otozuru, a female master of the form. Kusemai was performed mostly by women.

THE GION FESTIVAL

chigo, aboard the floats as mediums for the gods. Today the music is more important to inspire festival visitors and the *hikiko,* men who pull the floats[28] in the processions on July 17 and 24.

Byōbu Matsuri

Local families and businesses get in on the Gion Festival spirit of generosity by sharing their family heirlooms with the public in a sub-festival called the **Byōbu Matsuri** (Folding-Screen Festival). As you walk along the streets, keep your eyes open for window displays, or discreetly open doorways with priceless folding screens, kimono, *ikebana* flower arrangements, and other fine arts on display.

Fortunately for us, some families are deeply committed to the Byōbu Matsuri, like some in the **Kita Kannon Yama** *neighborhood.*

What to display to the public, if anything, is entirely at their discretion. Feel free to reciprocate their hospitality with a smile, wave, "thank you," or even a bow. You might make some new friends, or at least warm some hearts.

The byōbu folding screens may depict features of the seasons, battles, animals, dragons, or scenes of the

---

[28] See the section on **Tsuji Mawashi Corner Turning** for more on the role of hikiko.

Gion Festival itself. The latter are important sources of information for Gion Festival history.

*Folding screens showing Kyoto townscapes (and the Gion Festival) like this one formerly in the **Hachiman Yama** neighborhood are important references for our understanding of the city and festival. Unfortunately, this historic home has been sold to a Tokyo buyer and now stands empty, its future uncertain. Showing our support for the remaining **Byōbu Matsuri** and Kyoto **townscape conservation** may encourage them to continue.*

VISITING THE GION FESTIVAL

A month of rituals, five processions, countless deities, shrines and portable shrines, thirty-four **floats**, antique **treasures** and fine arts, otherworldly **music**, an array of **spiritual traditions**, family **heirlooms** on display, **kimono**, people watching, thousands of dedicated volunteers, more than 1150 years of **history**—the Gion Festival is truly a world-class celebration.

It also takes place in the subtropics in midsummer: it's hot as blazes, very humid, and prone to pouring rain, even typhoons. Add a very foreign language and a million visitors in an area less than a mile square.

Now you have a sense of the scope of your potential explorations.

Enjoying Your Visit

The Gion Festival is an unparalleled sensory experience, appropriately supernatural. The juxtaposition of sublime artistic detail with modern kitsch is wonderfully absurd. And the mundane surroundings can be chaotic. So relax, surrender to the climate and crowds, and savor whatever interests you.

*Yoiyoiyama, less crowded than **yoiyama**.*

At some point, the heat, crowds, noise, humidity, and fatigue may mix with the elaborate festival decorations and music, and you may feel as though you're being transported to another realm. Especially if you have a beer or *sake*. Keep in mind that this is a Shintō festival and Shintō is a kind of shamanism, very concerned with purification of the spirit and connection with the unseen world. If you're at the Gion Festival, on some level you're participating in the purification rituals. These are designed and offered to share benefits, with everyone present, with the deities and spirits, and with all beings everywhere. How amazing is that?

*A **yamabushi** or nature-mystic Buddhist monk, in a ritual for world peace at **En-no-Gyōja Yama**.*

Some Gion Festival participants consider it an ascetic practice. Sometimes I do too. This has some stressful aspects. To help you relieve those, I've shared some **practical tips** at the end of the book. I learned most of them the hard way, and sincerely hope that you can skip or at least decrease that part.

PLANNING YOUR VISIT

There are two major parts of the Gion Festival. One is lesser-known, but significant and rewarding in its cultural and spiritual richness. It centers around the **Yasaka Shrine** and is located at the eastern end of Shijō street (see **Maps**).

*The **mikoshi** are at the heart of ritual preparations at Yasaka Shrine.*

The other major part, far better known, focuses on the spectacular **yamaboko floats**. The floats' neighborhoods radiate out from the Shijō-Shinmachi intersection, west of the Shijō Karasuma subway station. Each float and neighborhood is unique, and each of their deities is

*Warrior monks illustrate an incredible historical battle scene at **Jōmyō Yama**.*

accompanied by fascinating myths and legends. The pages dedicated to each **float** will shed light on this for you.

Below is a high-level view of the different parts of the Gion Festival. After that, the **Explorations** section describes details about specific activities. If you prefer to plan by date, and for the most detail (including lesser-known events), see the daily **schedule** that appears towards the end of this book.

Note that activities are determined each year by each float's **chōnai** *neighborhood and* **Yasaka Shrine**, *and are subject to change.*

Yasaka Shrine

This is the spiritual center of the Gion Festival, as well as a pleasant place for a stroll: it turns into a beautiful park as you go up the mountainside. See the **Spiritual Roots** section to learn more.

Omukae Chōchin Lantern Procession

On July 10, to prepare the city streets for the portable *mikoshi* shrines' ritual bathing later the same night (see below), float musicians walk along Shijō street

in costume, carrying lanterns and playing music, departing **Yasaka Shrine** at 16:30. They are followed by children in delightful costumes

THE GION FESTIVAL

and painted faces, some of whom also participate in the **Hanagasa Junkō** (Flower Umbrella Procession) on July 24. They all walk west along Shijō street, turn north and walk up Kawaramachi street to City Hall. The children dance at City Hall around 17:30. Everyone returns to Yasaka Shrine, and then the Mikoshi Arai (below) takes place. When the mikoshi return around 21:00, the children **dance** again on one of Yasaka Shrine's two stages.

Mikoshi Arai Portable Shrine Purification

This ritual bathing of the portable *mikoshi* shrines prepares them for the **Yasaka Shrine deities** to enter them on the night of July 15 (see **Schedule**) for the **shinkōsai**. The mikoshi and their guild members depart Yasaka Shrine at 19:00 carrying giant fire torches. The mikoshi are ritually cleansed with river water (blessed earlier in the day) around 20:00 on Shijō bridge, over the Kamo River. After returning to Yasaka Shrine, children from the Mukae Chochin (above) **dance** there. A closing mikoshi arai takes place at the same times on July 28.

Shinkōsai: The Deities' Good Fortune Procession

The shinkōsai takes place on the evening of July 17. The **yamaboko floats**' procession that morning prepares the city streets for the coming of the Yasaka Shrine deities in the **mikoshi** during the shinkōsai. The yamaboko floats' procession is grand, stately, and—at least to the casual onlooker—mostly men. In contrast, much of the shinkōsai and kankōsai are boisterous and macho, though curiously very family-oriented too, as wives and kids are in clear view. Even though the shinkōsai and kankōsai form the spiritual heart of the Gion Festival, relatively few tourists attend.

Yochō, men who carry the mikoshi, prepare for the shinkōsai at Yasaka Shrine.

From about 16:00, **shinkōsai rituals** begin inside the Yasaka Shrine to prepare to carry the **mikoshi** from its stone steps on Shijō street (18:00). Each *mikoshi* goes on a different roundabout route to the *otabisho* or "honorable visiting place" at the Shijō-Teramachi intersection. Along the way, a *mikoshi* purifies the neighborhoods it travels through, creating a sacred space safe from harm.

If you'd like to experience the shinkōsai, it's easiest to start from Yasaka Shrine at the beginning and accompany the procession. Alternatively you can meet them towards the end along Kawaramachi street, between Sanjō and Shijō streets, and follow them to the otabisho, where it all finishes. The mikoshi and

THE GION FESTIVAL

their guilds arrive at the *otabisho* between 21:00 and 23:00. Access an interactive map of the mikoshi routes at GionFestival.org.

Kankōsai: The Return Good Fortune Procession

On July 24, the yochō and other men with ceremonial roles begin departing the otabisho on the south side of the Shijō-Teramachi intersection around 16:20—each **mikoshi** and its guild depart and arrive at staggered times. Similar to the **shinkōsai**, each mikoshi is transported on its own route (access an interactive map via GionFestival. org). However, between 20:00 and 22:00, all three get carried along Sanjō street from Ōmiya to Teramachi street, and then south to Shijō and east to Higashiōji street. It can be good fun to follow along.

Musicians in ritual costume during the kankōsai.

They all arrive back at Yasaka Shrine between 22:00 and 23:00. After that, the deities' spirits are mysteriously transported from the mikoshi back to the shrine in a ritual in darkness. See the **Spiritual Roots** section for more on the **kankōsai**.

Hanagasa Junkō: The Flower Umbrella Procession

Over the centuries various Kyotoites have participated in the Gion Festival in diverse ways. As mentioned,

Yasaka Shrine is the regional shrine for the Gion neighborhood, which is famous for its *geiko-san*, a name that includes both accomplished geisha and their apprentices, known as *maiko*.

Geisha districts are also called *hanamachi* or "flower towns," and some of the earliest Gion Festival floats were large umbrellas. So it's natural that this procession consists of *hanagasa,* or flower umbrellas.

Gion geiko-san in the Hanagasa Junkō procession.

There are four hanamachi in the Gion district, and they alternate so that two participate in the Hanagasa Junkō each year. This event was introduced in 1966, some years after an earlier (and more elaborate) procession of geiko-san and kabuki actors had ceased due to financial constraints.[29] Despite its newness, some believe that the Hanagasa Junkō resembles the earliest Gion Festival processions. We know that in ancient times all the processions included more dancing and diverse forms of participation, such as performing noh theater on the floats.

Compared to the Yamaboko Junkō procession, the Hanagasa Junkō is more feminine in nature. Besides geiko-san, it features musicians, children, and others in colorful costumes. The Hanagasa Junkō

---

[29] Special thanks to Mr. Takashi Shimada for his outstanding research and awareness-raising of this earlier procession, and of the Gion Festival in general.

shows us how **performing arts** have always been central to Shintō rituals.

The Hanagasa Junkō starts at 10:00 on July 24 from the front steps of Yasaka Shrine. Yes, this means it's held at the same

Lovely young traditional dancers form part of the Hanagasa Junkō.

time as the *yamaboko* floats procession. After returning to Yasaka Shrine around noon, they perform throughout the afternoon on the shrine's central stage, as an offering to the Gion Festival deities. Some of the dances they perform are hundreds of years old. See **Maps** for the procession route.

Yamaboko Floats

Strictly speaking, the role of the **yamaboko floats** is to welcome and bid farewell to the all-important **Yasaka Shrine deities**. However, for the vast majority of people, the floats are the stars of the Gion Festival. When people think "Gion Festival," the floats are what come to mind.

*There's no sight quite like the yamaboko floats processions. Here, the **Ato Matsuri** procession on July 24.*

The Gion Festival **neighborhoods**

display their **floats** in two parts: the larger and extraordinarily popular *Saki Matsuri* ("early festival" from July 10-17), and the smaller-scale and more subdued *Ato Matsuri* ("later festival" from July 18-24). Note that the first two days are primarily occupied with **float construction** and *hikizome* test pulls. A few floats' treasure display areas begin opening in the evening of July 12 and 20, with more joining in subsequent days.

EXPLORATIONS: WHAT TO SEE AND DO AT THE GION FESTIVAL

Float Construction: *Yamaboko Tate*

We can think of the Gion Festival as a gigantic mandala. Tibetan Buddhist sand mandalas are painstakingly created, then soon swept away. Similarly, each year, the Gion Festival gets created in all its magnificence, its bare parts assembled and brought to life. Within just one week the mandala then gets dismantled, and is gone until the following year.

Japanese culture has a famous philosophy called *mono-no-aware,* a thoughtful appreciation

*Finishing touches at **Kikusui Boko** and **Niwatori Boko**.*

of the fleeting beauty of this world. Every moment we experience mono-no-aware, and every July we experience it on a huge scale with the Gion Festival.

On July 10-12, and then again on July 18-20, we can watch each chōnai neighborhood build their part of the huge mandala. Each float starts with just a few timbers simply lashed together with ropes. The complexity and beauty expand from there, moment by moment. Not a single nail is used, and safety is paramount: an unstable float would be devastating. Watch the artistry of the carpenters at work[30] and you will never look at rope and timber the same way again.

Human power and pulleys get **Niwatori Boko's** *frame upright. See how yamaboko tate is built into the city street.*

Transmitted down many generations, the rope-tying techniques, called *nawa-garami*, provide both strength and flexibility. The larger floats each require more than five kilometers or three miles of rope. Different knots have distinctive names, such as crane, shrimp, or butterfly knots. Some floats use modern mechanization to assist them and add safety, whereas others still do it entirely by hand,

---

[30] In centuries past the carpenters were laborers from different towns that had historical associations with respective chōnai. Nowadays the carpenters are professionals, and the hoko chōnai in particular rely on them for their specialized knowledge and skill, central to the safety and success of the Gion Festival.

THE GION FESTIVAL

the traditional way, with neighborhood men heaving the central pine tree mast vertical.

The Gion Festival is so important to Kyoto that construction and mobility considerations are built into the city infrastructure. Shijō's street lights, for example, swivel on hinges to let the floats pass.

The hoko's central pole is called a *shingi,* a "god's tree," and can be up to 20 meters tall. It acts as a kind of lightning rod to attract the attention of the deities in the heavens, and transport them down to street level where they may mingle among us in Kyoto.

Adding a one-ton wooden wheel to **Iwatō Yama**.

About twenty people must lift the larger floats with levers in order to be able to coax the wheels onto their hubs.

Next the chōnai decorate their floats. We get to watch the mandala come into its glory. The floats and their treasures are like gigantic jigsaw puzzles. Everything has to be put together in the precisely correct place and order, or it doesn't work. One festival patron told me how, after two hours of preparation, someone realized something had been done out of order early on. It took them four hours to undo and fix it again. That they build the largest floats in a day is extraordinary.

An incredible amount of detail goes into building and decorating each float. **Kankō Boko** *(above) and* **Hashi Benkei Yama** *(right).*

TREASURE VIEWING

The **Saki Matsuri** floats' treasures begin going on view from the evening of July 12 for the largest floats, with all of them on view from the 14th to the 16th. For the **Ato Matsuri**, **Ōfune Boko** and **Minami Kannon Yama** open their treasure displays on the 21st, with other floats following on the 22nd and 23rd. Chances are good that you won't see so many museum-quality treasures so close up anywhere else on the planet. There are many diverse experiences to enjoy, so don't spend time waiting in lines—move on. Every float has a treasure

Gilt roof interior panels await installation at **Naginata Boko**. *The brief yamaboko tate float construction time frame is an important opportunity for documentation and research, as the treasures are generally only out of storage once a year.*

display area, and float patrons, neighborhood residents, and volunteers proudly stand by to share and support your enjoyment.

The practice of providing detailed, well-researched labeling of objects on display is not part of the Gion Festival tradition, though it is becoming more common, almost entirely in Japanese. Comment on my Gion Festival social media channels if you'd like to learn more about float treasures in English. Which ones, and what would you like to know? I'm happy to share what I know.

*An abundance of treasures at **Hachiman Yama's** display area.*

Be forewarned that the "display" areas were not originally designed as such. They are more like a combination of shrine, meeting place, and staging station. As you'll see when you visit these places, each float's deity and sacred objects are revered here until they're mounted on the floats for the processions on July 17 and 24. Until then, neighborhood supporters come to pay their respects to the deities, prepare the float treasures for the processions, and enjoy socializing. We are all

*Sumptuous golden 18th-century Mughal embroidery and a "seven treasures" woven net decoration at **Taishi Yama**.*

graciously invited to join in. Our Gion Festival hosts may get the prize for the greatest amount of hospitality per square meter.

For the smaller floats, entrance is free. If you're looking for souvenirs or feeling hungry or thirsty, small purchases at the floats help support the communities' ability to keep sharing this way with people like us. Some of the larger floats require a purchase (¥1000-2000) to enter their treasure display area and board their float. Is it worth it? Yes, at least once. See the section on **Boarding a Hoko or Yama**.

Byōbu Matsuri: Folding Screen Festival

Visiting the Gion Festival also includes a delightful sub festival called the *Byōbu Matsuri*, or "folding screen festival." Neighborhood families and companies display works of historic and artistic value—such as folding screens—and other heirlooms. By voluntarily displaying these during the festival, these families and companies generously give us a taste of the culture that kimono merchants traditionally enjoyed.

A local textile business gets into the spirit of the Byōbu Matsuri.

Originally, local families and businesses displayed art treasures as a way to welcome honored guests during the Gion Festival. Some still do this. It's also a way for the residents and companies to connect with the public, as well as their guests. We may not get to be a special guest, but we still benefit from the beauty.

Recently, households and companies are getting more creative with the Byōbu Matsuri. Some display more modern art, or handmade crafts.

These displays are randomly spread out around central Kyoto, so the best thing to do is to keep your eyes open as you walk around. Since presenting these treasures to the public is discretionary, displays and dates can vary. Some beautiful displays I have seen only once and never again.

A miniature procession is part of Byōbu Matsuri.

That said, the **Kita Kannon Yama** and **Hachiman Yama** chōnai neighborhood communities are renowned for their generous and beautiful presentations during the **Ato Matsuri**. The Ato Matsuri is smaller than the **Saki Matsuri**, but its Byōbu Matsuri tradition has always been stronger. Head north of Shijō on Shinmachi street, particularly between Nishiki-kōji and Sanjō streets.

Some of the byōbu can be easily enjoyed for their universal beauty. Others we savor more

*Byōbu Matsuri in the **Kita Kannon Yama** chōnai.*

with a bit of context. Calligraphy is appreciated for the expression of the character and mindstate of the painter at the time of painting, more than the meaning of the words. Imagine a highly trained monk focusing on expressing his realization through the brush. Some byōbu are upcycled from other artwork, such as smaller *ukiyo-e* woodblock prints. Others show a famous scene, perhaps a meeting of poets, or a battle. Japanese people may recognize these instantly, or there may be a small description in Japanese. Feel free to ask someone nearby what it's about if you'd like to learn more.

I saw this lovely byōbu once and never again, probably because we viewers didn't practice the Golden Rule. This is one good reason why now I do.

These treasures are privately owned, and considerable effort goes into conserving and setting up the displays. It's considerate of us to practice the Golden Rule, acting in ways we'd like people to act in and around our homes. And if you see a resident or volunteer, try expressing your appreciation—it is often warmly accepted.

Traditional Architecture: *Kyōmachiya*

Downtown Kyoto is famous for its **kyōmachiya**, traditional Kyoto townhouses. As downtown real estate values climb, some chōnai residents demonstrate an

THE GION FESTIVAL

incredible commitment to the festival and traditional culture by resolutely conserving these buildings.

Compared to other cultural capitals in developed countries, Kyoto and Japan have been slow to provide support for the conservation of their traditional cityscapes. Fortunately, there's a growing cityscape conservation movement in Kyoto, which is gaining more traction. Showing your appreciation for these buildings and their conservation efforts may help strengthen their commitment. See the pages on **Minami Kannon Yama** and **Ōfune Boko** for success stories.

*Several traditional kyōmachiya beautify the **Tokusa Yama chōnai**.*

Part of the beauty of traditional Kyoto architecture is in the details.

Kaisho: Floats' Treasure Display Buildings

Some floats have lost their traditional *kaisho*—buildings for community gatherings and treasure displays—in major Kyoto fires, or to economic and real estate development pressures. The Gion Festival floats' remaining *kyōmachiya*, traditional Kyoto townhouses, can be grouped into roughly four types:

1) A courtyard lined with rooms/display space, opening up at the end of a narrow walkway. These are cool and quiet even on a hot, busy day, and are some of my favorite festival sites to relax at.
2) A two-story "display machiya" townhouse designed to display the float's deity from the second story to the populace below. The treasures are shown on the ground floor.
3) A two-story "float machiya" townhouse built with a large room facing the street on the second floor, from where we can cross a walkway to board the larger floats.
4) All of these buildings usually feature a fourth type of structure, a traditional white-plastered *kura* storehouse, at their rear. The thick-walled *kura* are fireproof and, amazingly,

*The long, cool entry walkway at **Arare Tenjin Yama** invites us into its lovely courtyard display area.*

*The display machiya at **Yamabushi Yama** uses architecture to keep the deity above our heads as a sign of respect. Visitors can enjoy the treasures below.*

possess museum-quality conservation conditions, optimal for storing Gion Festival treasures.

Below is a list of floats that are still housed in traditional buildings. In addition, two floats' chōnai communities have built beautiful modern replicas of traditional machiya buildings, indicated below. Also noted are which floats can be boarded by members of the public.

There are other traditional buildings—private residential and business buildings with historic connections to the Gion Festival. Some of these are open to the public to varying degrees. Their locations are near the floats marked with an asterisk.

*We can board **Ōfune Boko** on a bridge from the second story of its float machiya. Note the bamboo lattice used in the **hoko tate** construction.*

*The thick white walls of **Urade Yama's** kura storehouse.*

Architecture, Saki Matsuri (July 12-17)

- **Arare Tenjin Yama** – Courtyard.
- **Ayagasa Boko** – Small courtyard; Shintō shrine.
- **Fune Boko** – Float machiya replica,* can board (fee). *Visit the Nagae-Ke residence across the street (fee). Details below.
- **Hakuga Yama** – Residential machiya.* *Visit the Sugimoto-Ke residence (fee). The entrance is in the same building, next door. Details below.
- **Hōka Boko** – Float machiya; men can board.
- **Hoshō Yama** – Display machiya.
- **Mōsō Yama** – Courtyard.
- **Taishi Yama** – Residential machiya* *If permitted (varies by year), view some of the Hata-Ke residence. Details below.
- **Tsuki Boko** – Float machiya; can board (fee).
- **Urade Yama** – Courtyard; Shintō shrine.
- **Yamabushi Yama** – Display machiya.

*Preparing for **hoko tate** inside **Ayagasa Boko's** shrine display area.*

***Hoshō Yama**'s deity overlooks its float from the second floor of its display machiya.*

THE GION FESTIVAL

Private Residences

As mentioned, conservation culture and legal instruments to support conservation of private homes have been relatively slow to arrive in Kyoto. As a result, these buildings are unusual and extremely valuable.

- *Nagae-Ke* is the former home of the Nagae family, across the street from the **Fune Boko** *kaisho* display area. It was recently purchased by a real estate development company, which has expressed interest in preserving it as a showcase of traditional Kyoto architecture. Given that they have built several large apartment buildings in the area in recent years, this is a promising new direction for the company. If you value their new interest in architectural conservation, let them know. Your input may help conserve Nagae Ke. The late Mr. Nagae was one of the visionaries who helped Fune Boko and its treasures join the digital revolution, a bold move in such an ancient festival. July 14-16, 10:00-20:00, last entrance at 19:30. ¥700 for adults, ¥600 for students, ¥300 for junior high school students. Younger children free.
- *Sugimoto-Ke* is the largest kyōmachiya in the entire city, and home to the tenth generation of the Sugimoto family. If you're a culture buff or love architecture,

The Sugimoto-Ke facade at **Hakuga Yama**.

be sure to visit this beautiful home. Built in 1870, it's modeled after the previous residence, built on this site in 1767 but destroyed by the Great Genji Fire of 1864. Here we can get a sense of how their family has lived at the heart of the Gion Festival for generations: **Hakuga Yama**'s treasures have been displayed inside their home since the 1940s. The family art collection is exquisite and is rotated three times during the Gion Festival. Use the Golden Rule: imagine how you would want people to behave when visiting your home. We support ongoing conservation with the ¥800-1500 entry fee. July 10-12, 13:00-17:00 / July 14, 16:30-21:00; July 15-16, 10:30-21:00. The artwork is changed on the 13th and again for the Ato Matsuri exhibit 7/21-23 (see below). Confirm days and times on their website: http://en.sugimotoke.or.jp

- Depending on the year, **Taishi Yama**'s treasures may be displayed inside the impressive **Hata-Ke**, a refined traditional home from 1869. http://www.hata-ke.jp/about/ (Japanese only).

*Hata-Ke at **Taishi Yama**.*

THE GION FESTIVAL

Architecture, Ato Matsuri (July 19-24)

- **En-no-Gyōja Yama** – Courtyard.
- **Hachiman Yama** – Courtyard; Shintō shrine; private machiya (Byōbu Matsuri) nearby.
- **Hashi Benkei Yama** – Display machiya.
- **Kita Kannon Yama** – Float machiya; private machiya (Byōbu Matsuri) nearby.
- **Koi Yama** – Courtyard.
- **Minami Kannon Yama** – Replica machiya, beautifully restored neighborhood.
- **Ōfune Boko** – Float machiya; can board (fee)
- **Suzuka Yama** – Machiya.

*At the end of a long, narrow entryway, **Koi Yama's** kaisho is cool and quiet.*

Private Residences

- Visit the beautiful Sugimoto-Ke, open for a special viewing to the public. The family art treasures on display are different from during the Saki Matsuri: July 21-23, 13:00-18:00. The ¥800-1500 entry fee goes towards ongoing conservation. Confirm days and times on their website: http://en.sugimoto-ke.or.jp

Boarding Yamaboko

Most of the larger floats allow visitors to board, usually for a small fee or purchase. The proceeds go towards ongoing conservation. Try to go early, as later in the day and week you may need to wait longer in line. The Gion Festival is such a vast and varied experience; it may be better to move on or return later than to wait in line. Also note that dates and times you can board different floats vary.

Enjoy looking closely: there is a lot happening under the floats' roof peaks. Magnificent sculpture, paintings, and metalwork at **Tsuki Boko**.

At all the floats, boarding gives you a chance to look at the textiles, woodcarving, and metalwork details up close. Be sure to look under the roof peak and eaves. This is the best craftsmanship Kyoto has had to offer for centuries.

Enjoying the view of Kyoto streets from inside a float, peeking through the *chōchin* lanterns, is a sight you'll remember for the rest of your life. If you board a float at night, you may be able to share the extremely tight space with some performing *gionbayashi* festival musicians (follow the **music** to find them). It will

THE GION FESTIVAL

give you a sense of their amazing concentration under challenging conditions.

Floats whose interiors are especially interesting (notably the ceiling inside the float) are marked with an asterisk. Note that the wait to board these will likely be longer. Fees go towards conservation.

Boarding Floats During the Saki Matsuri (July 13-16)

- **Fune Boko*** – See beautiful gilt paintings of flowers on ceiling compartments.
- **Hōka Boko** – Men only.
- **Iwatō Yama**
- **Kankō Boko**
- **Kikusui Boko** – ¥2000 fee includes **tea ceremony**, tea sweet, and souvenir dish.
- **Naginata Boko*** – Men only. See Asian astronomical configurations on the ceiling. Expect long lines.
- **Niwatori Boko**
- **Tsuki Boko*** – See gilt paintings on the ceiling, showing scenes from the novel *Tale of the Genji* on fans (see **Art Treasures**).

Enjoying the view from ***Naginata Boko***.

Boarding Floats During the Ato Matsuri (July 19-24)

- **Minami Kannon Yama**
- **Ōfune Boko**

Hikizome: Pull a Yama or Hoko

Saki Matsuri *Hikizome*

Niwatori Boko's hikizome is pulled by young women from the Ikenobo Junior College next door.

Incredibly, you too may pull one of the gigantic Gion Matsuri floats. Two *hikizome* or test pulls take place during the **Saki Matsuri**, to make sure that everything about the float construction is in working order. It's good fun, but intense: expect crowds and arrive early if you'd like a place. Take care, particularly of small children and the elderly. No photos while pulling—it's genuinely dangerous.

On July 12, the hoko on Shijō and Muromachi streets each hold a trial *hikizome* pull that is open to public participation. The floats' hikizome go in order, one right after another. **Kankō Boko** begins on Shijō street at 14:00, followed by **Tsuki Boko** (also on Shijō), then **Niwatori Boko** on Muromachi street next door, together with **Kikusui Boko** on Muromachi, and then **Naginata Boko** east on Shijō street.

THE GION FESTIVAL

Niwatori Boko and **Kikusui Boko** are less crowded.

The floats are so close to one another that some people, lovers of chaos, try to pull several of them in turn. The whole thing is over within a few hours.

On July 13 starting at 15:00, **Iwatō Yama**, **Fune Boko**, and **Hōka Boko** on Shinmachi street have a hikizome test pull that is open to the public, too. They all move

Kikusui Boko and *Kankō Boko* hikizome on Shijō street.

a block north and south on Shinmachi street, simultaneously. Expect crowds, arrive a bit early, and take care for your physical safety.

Ato Matsuri *Hikizome*

On July 20 from 14:30, the **Ato Matsuri** hikizome takes place on Shinmachi street, with **Ōfune Boko**, **Minami Kannon Yama**, and **Kita Kannon Yama** all moving simultaneously. The Ato Matsuri is generally quieter and less crowded than the

Kids participate in hikizome on Shinmachi street. You just know they're going to remember this for the rest of their lives.

Saki Matsuri, so their hikizome is too.

Tea Ceremony

Kikusui Boko, July 14-16, ¥2,000 at the time of writing. Tea ceremony times vary according to the day and year but are roughly 12:00-22:00. Please confirm the days and times at the float.[31] It includes a demonstration of tea ceremony by alternating tea schools, a bowl of matcha green tea (high in caffeine and antioxidants), a tea sweet, and a lovely souvenir tea dish. Plus air conditioning and a place to sit and enjoy looking at some float treasures. See the **Kikusui Boko** float's pages to learn of its historic association with tea ceremony.

Delicious, beautiful, and refreshing. That time the souvenir dish was in the shape of a chrysanthemum.

Dance and Music

- On July 10, float musicians play *gionbayashi music* in the *Omukae Chōchin* lantern procession beginning at 14:30 from **Yasaka Shrine**. They're followed by children in costume who perform lovely dances at City Hall from 15:30. The children dance again at Yasaka Shrine from

---

[31] Subscribe to my Gion Festival social media channels for timely updates.

around 21:00, after the **Mikoshi Arai** ritual on Shijō Bridge.

*Young girls perform a Sagi Mai Heron Dance at **Yasaka Shrine**.*

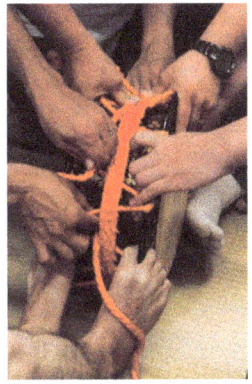

Tuning a Gionbayashi taikō *drum.*

- *Gion Bayashi:* **Gion Festival music,** played on the larger floats from 18:00, July 12-17 and July 20-23. On the eve of July 12, **Kankō Boko** and **Kikusui Boko** start playing the distinctive gionbayashi, joined each night by more of the large floats. All of the large floats play during **yoiyoiyoiyama**, **yoiyoiyama**, and **yoiyama**, after 18:00 on July 14-16. You can board some of the floats while the ohayashi troupes are playing music. You'll be amazed at their concentration under the cramped conditions. Up to 50 people ride and play music together on a single float during the July 17 and 24 processions. Some have told me that they tie small boys to posts with rope around their waist to keep them safe. Others say that it's not necessary, since the crowdedness itself keeps everyone in place.

*Happily packed in at **Kikusui Boko**.*

- *Kami Asobi* (God-Pleasing) dance and music, July 14, 18:00 and 19:00, **Iwatō Yama**. Though not a Gion Festival tradition, you can enjoy this beautiful traditional Shintō-style dance with pleasing traditional flute and bell, and *taiko* drum rhythms that will make you want to join in. Free, and small purchase at Iwatō Yama encouraged. Expect crowds.
- **Ayagasa Boko**'s lively ancient style music and stick-twirling dance (Gion Bayashi and *Bō-furi* Bayashi). July 14 and 15, music starts from 18:40 followed by the dance from 19:00, then repeats every hour until and including 22:00. On July 16, the music begins at 18:10 and the dance at 18:30, and

repeats every hour up to and including 20:30. The stick-twirling was an ancient method of expelling harmful spirits, like a shaman's rattle. Expect crowds.

- Children's Warabe-Mai Kami Asobi Dance, July 15, 18:00, **Iwatō Yama**. Local school children join in the festival spirit with this cute group dance.

- Iwami Kagura, July 16, 18:30-21:00 at Yasaka Shrine. A dynamic traditional dance-theater from western Japan featuring dramatic movements and spectacular costumes. It was traditionally performed to please Shintō gods  (we humans get to enjoy it, too). The general themes celebrate gods defeating demons, and Yasaka Shrine and Gion Festival deities and legends. Expect crowds.

- Traditional Japanese dance and music (various), Yasaka Shrine, July 24, approximately 12:30-17:30. After participating in the **Hanagasa Junkō** (Flower Umbrella Procession), *geiko-san* (apprentice and master geisha) and other artists and their apprentices take turns **performing arts** on Yasaka Shrine's stage.

Noh Theater

Noh theater is everywhere and nowhere in the Gion Festival. A noh stage is at the heart of the **Yasaka Shrine**, home to the Gion Festival deities. Gion Festival **yamaboko floats**' sacred statues and themes relate to no less than 16 noh plays. Some of these were written by the 14th-century genius noh playwright Zeami,[32] who we know attended the Gion Festival and watched live actors perform on festival floats.

Noh plays are profound studies of human nature, often concerning transformative relationships between the seen and unseen worlds.

Many sacred statues wear exquisite noh costumes, and are dressed each year by professional noh actors. Why noh performance itself has disappeared from the Gion Festival remains a mystery.

The sacred statue of the goddess Suzuka wears a noh costume, noh mask, and holds a folding fan used in noh theater.
Suzuka Yama.

Museums

The Museum of Kyoto often puts on Gion Festival-related exhibits during the month of July, showing treasures that we might not otherwise see. Descriptions are often available only in Japanese, so

---

[32] See **Ashikari Yama** and **Tokusa Yama** for more on Zeami.

THE GION FESTIVAL

if you have a Japanese friend willing to accompany you, that could make it more interesting for both of you. Check the museum's **website**: bunpaku.or.jp/en/ Kudos to the museum for having some information available in eight languages.

KYOTO'S MASSIVE HISTORIC STREET PARTIES: *YOIYOIYOIYAMA, YOIYOIYAMA, AND YOIYAMA*

Yoi means "eve," so *yoiyoiyoiyama* is on July 14 and July 21, three eves before the great processions on July 17 and 24. Yoiyoiyama is on the 15th and 22nd, and yoiyama is on July 16 and 23. From 18:00 until 23:00 during the **Saki Matsuri** (July 14-16), central Kyoto streets[33] are closed to traffic and full of festival-goers instead.[34]

*The iconic festival lanterns and mythical creatures lend an air of mystique at **Mōsō Yama**.*

These evenings are for lovers of crowds, unusual street food, and people-watching: masses of people wander through the center of the Gion Festival to enjoy the food, hear the music, see the floats and their treasures, and revel in the sensory overload.

---

[33] It's a large area: from Horikawa street in the west to Yasaka Shrine in the east, and from Takatsuji street in the south to Sanjō street in the north.

[34] The streets are closed off with signs that read, "Pedestrian Paradise" in Japanese. It's one of my favorite festival terms.

*Yoiyama at **Mōsō Yama** early on, before the crowds.*

All treasure display areas are open during this time. Each consecutive night attracts more visitors, particularly if it falls on a weekend. The outlying floats' neighborhoods are still relatively quiet and pleasant for an evening stroll.

The **Ato Matsuri** is more subdued and thus more like the Gion Festival of yesteryear. Some people love the *yatai* street and game stalls, but some find them tacky—they're not allowed in the Ato Matsuri.

During the **Saki Matsuri** in particular,

This Saki Matsuri yatai *food stall offers traditional* ayu *sweetfish cooked over charcoal. Get in the spirit by eating something you've never had before.*

*The mellower **Ato Matsuri** yoiyama, from **Ōfune Boko**.*

it is possible (even likely) to get stuck in the crowds and not be able to regulate your schedule or direction. It may be helpful to have a backup plan in case you miss a rendezvous.

THE *YAMABOKO* FLOATS

The Gion Festival's 34 *yamaboko* floats are arguably the most famous thing about the festival. But in fact, the Gion Festival's true luminaries are the many deities to which the entire celebration is dedicated. Maybe you can sense them, but deities are generally invisible. So the festival's spectacular yamaboko capture most of our worldly attention.

What do you need to know about the Gion Festival yamaboko?

Four hoko floats wait at the Shijō-Karasuma intersection to begin the Saki Matsuri procession on July 17.

Firstly, the yamaboko appear in two phases. Twenty-three take part in the larger **Saki Matsuri** ("early festival," from July 10-17). Another 11 floats participate in the mellower **Ato Matsuri** ("later festival," from July 18-24). During this time, the yamaboko floats and their distinctive lanterns beautify the area around the Shijō-Karasuma intersection.[35]

Secondly, yamaboko come in two types: *yama* and *hoko*. These are described below.

Thirdly, each yama and each hoko organizes around its own deity or deities and their legends and myths, or some other kind of spiritual-cultural theme. See the subsequent pages on each float for more details on their fascinating stories.

Yama and Hoko Floats Explained

How big are the yamaboko? In general—though not always—the hoko are much larger, multi-storied floats. Weighing up to 12 tons, up to 50 volunteer men called *hikiko* pull them through Kyoto streets using thick, long ropes. *Hoko* means "pike" and dates back to the Gion Festival **origins**, when participants carried pikes in procession. Six of the ten hoko feature an elaborate central pole adorned with various ornaments as their crowning glory. It's now called a *shingi* or "deities' tree." The

*The **Niwatori Boko** team prepares for the July 17 procession. Note its striking* shingi.

---

[35] Meanwhile, in the same time frames, parallel celebrations are held at **Yasaka Shrine**, in the easternmost part of the Gion neighborhood. These are mostly rituals and offerings to the shrine's resident deities, the main deities of the Gion Festival.

THE GION FESTIVAL

shingi is a kind of celestial lightning rod, connecting beings on heaven and earth. Since it's believed that Shintō *kami* spirits travel down the shingi during the festival, these hoko don't enshrine a separate deity like the yama do. Each shingi has a unique symbol on top.

Generally, the 23 *yama* are smaller than the hoko. Instead of a shingi, they usually feature a pine tree as their connector to the heavenly element. A few use a different kind of tree, such as plum, cedar, or cherry blossom, and two feature a bridge instead (since trees don't grow on bridges).

Ashikari Yama, *illustrating a scene from the noh play, "The Reed Cutter." Note the pine tree and contemporary textiles.*

Most yama are rolled on wheels by groups of men holding shoulder-level wooden supports. Traditionally many of them were stages, on which **noh theater** plays were performed. Noh has an ancient connection with Shintō and communicating between the seen and unseen worlds. Several of the yamaboko's themes today are still connected with noh plays.

Iwatō Yama, *one of the hiki-yama that looks like a hoko.*

But yamaboko don't simply make two tidy groups. Some of the yama are large, pulled with ropes, and generally look like hoko (such as **Iwatō Yama**, **Kita Kannon Yama**, and **Minami Kannon Yama**). These are called *hiki-yama*, meaning "pulled yama." Smaller yama carried on the shoulders are called *kaki-yama*, or "shoulder-borne yama."

*Three yama with different silhouettes in the July 24 **Ato Matsuri** procession.*

Some of the hoko are small and shaped like umbrellas (**Ayagasa Boko** and **Shijō Kasa Boko**). Others are shaped like boats (like **Fune Boko** below, and **Ōfune Boko**).

Each yamaboko provides us with an opportunity to experience the festival in a unique way. Typically,

the hoko are more opulent and the yama have a stronger community feeling. Locals have told me that before the Gion Festival got so famous (and busy), they would enjoy going around to the various floats and visiting one another for a cup of tea in the *kaisho* display areas. Some of the yama's treasure display areas still offer this kind of ambiance. Here, residents and visitors alike can enjoy the float's decorative treasures as well as one another's company.

Continue reading for details on the Saki Matsuri and **Ato Matsuri**, and on each individual float.

SAKI MATSURI: THE "EARLY FESTIVAL:" JULY 10-17

The Saki Matsuri literally builds up from July 10, with its floats, activity, and excitement growing until it peaks on July 17 with the procession of yamaboko floats.

Officially, the deities on each float travel through downtown Kyoto to prepare the streets for and welcome the arrival of the Yasaka Shrine deities. In the **shinkōsai** that same night, hundreds of men carry Yasaka Shrine's portable **mikoshi** shrines on their shoulders, bringing the deities to stay in central Kyoto[36] for a week.

The Saki Matsuri floats procession welcomes the Gion Festival deities downtown. **Ayagasa Boko** *in foreground.*

---

[36] The Yasaka Shrine deities stay at the *otabisho* "visiting place" at the Shijō-Teramachi intersection July 17-24, when they get carried back to Yasaka Shrine in the **kankōsai**.

Men take turns shouldering the mikoshi in the shinkōsai.

The **Ato Matsuri** and *kankōsai* are a similar process, in reverse, giving thanks and bidding the Yasaka Shrine deities farewell as they go back to their regular abode for another year.

THE SAKI MATSURI TIMELINE: OVERVIEW

Construction of the Saki Matsuri floats begins on July 10th. At this time, the *chōnai* communities related to the largest floats start building the great festival mandala. They begin with the five hoko on Shijō and

Muromachi streets, and then the three hoko and large yama on Shinmachi street (see **Maps**). The 15 smaller yamaboko join day by day, for 23 floats in total.

If you wonder what it takes to pull the gigantic floats, you can join in the *hikizome* test pulls on July 12 and 13.

From the night of July 12, treasure display areas for the largest hoko begin to open. Musicians play the distinctive **gionbayashi music** from the evenings—follow the sound. All the floats' treasures are on public display on July 14, 15, and 16, from about 9:00 until around 22:30. If you join the peak **yoiyoiyoiyama**,

THE GION FESTIVAL

yoiyoiyama, and yoiyama celebration on the nights of July 14-16, Shijō and Karasuma streets are closed to auto traffic from 18:00-23:00. Instead of cars, countless people walk along the streets, visiting food stalls, game stalls and Gion Festival floats.

From about 21:30 on July 16, the *Hiyori Kagura* (literally, "Good Weather Music for the Deities") ritual takes place. All the ohayashi **music** troupes and float patrons walk along Shijō street with paper lanterns to the *otabisho* "visiting place" at the Shijō-Teramachi intersection. There they pray to the **Yasaka Shrine deities** for good weather during the July 17 procession. They play music both as they go and as they return. **Naginata Boko**'s ohayashi and patrons walk all the way to **Yasaka Shrine** and back, an especially impressive undertaking for the young boys and elders in the community.

Each float's **chōnai** decides its schedule on its own, and as such everything is always subject to change. Enjoy the magical details,

Look up for more beauty.
Iwatō Yama.

*The **Hōka Boko** ohayashi getting ready to play music during **yoiyoiyoiyama**.*

follow your own interests, and use the **Practical Tips** at the end of this book to make the most of your explorations. However you find the crowds, the extraordinary stimuli of the festival and its many thousands of visitors are an unforgettable experience. See **Visiting the Gion Festival** and the **Schedule** sections for details.

The Saki Matsuri floats procession

July 17 brings the stately procession of 23 floats. From early in the morning, the floats prepare and begin lining up along both Shijō and Karasuma near their intersection. At 9:00, **Naginata Boko's** *chigo* child cuts the sacred rope across Shijō street west of Fuyacho street in the *shimenawa-kiri* ritual, thereby opening a sacred space for the procession to begin. Be forewarned that this intersection and event are very crowded. It may be more enjoyable to watch from a more spacious location later in the procession.[37]

Naginata Boko's chigo performs a ritual dance at the front of the float during the procession. **Hōka Boko**'s *sacred doll does a similar dance.*

By tradition, **Naginata Boko** is always the first hoko

---

[37] Kawaramachi street, midway between Shijō and Oike streets, may be one of the least crowded areas.

THE GION FESTIVAL

in the Saki Matsuri procession. The order is also predetermined for a few other floats, but most draw a number by lottery at the beginning of July, so every Gion Festival

Tsuki Boko's Kuji Aratame.

procession is unique by design. Each float pauses on Shijō street at Sakaimachi street to ritually present the number of its order in the procession to the city mayor in a ritual called *Kuji Aratame*, meaning "lottery confirmation."

At the beginning of the procession, each float begins to rumble and creak forward east along Shijō with the crisp excitement of initiating another grand Gion Festival procession. As the morning goes by, however, the sun, pavement, and people all heat up, or perhaps more rain falls. For most of the route, there's no shade. The largest floats weigh up to 12 tons, and no doubt feel heavier as the sun gets higher and the journey goes longer. The men's feet must surely ache.

After Kuji Aratame, **Hakuga Yama**'s *representative uses his fan to signal the float to proceed.*

Alongside the float, experienced and brave men called *kurumagata* place wooden wedges under the wheels to keep the floats going straight. A very risky job, they make it look easy.

The chōnai patrons walk in stately single-file lines, wearing their starched *kamishimo* costumes. At times, I have found this part of the procession uninteresting. As I've gotten to know the people, though,

*Feeling fresh before starting the procession at **Kikusui Boko**.*

and watched it repeatedly, I realize what an accomplishment it is

***Tōrō Yama** patrons just starting their three-hour walk; they will look this good at the end of it too.*

*Musicians are packed into **Fune Boko** together with four life-sized antique statues of their deities, waiting for tsuji mawashi.*

to still be walking straight and tall after three hours on the hot or wet pavement, a particularly challenging undertaking for small boys and seniors. Friends of mine have accomplished this test of endurance in their 80s.

Higher up on each float, up to 50 ohayashi musicians can be crammed into a space not much larger than the

THE GION FESTIVAL

interior of an SUV. The first time a festival elder told me that number, he must have seen the astonishment on my face, because he continued, "It's an ascetic practice, I'm telling you!"

They're basically stuck in position for three hours straight, playing **music** designed to move people in and out of altered states, with temperatures up to 40º C/ 100º F and rainy-season humidity. In short, it's ancient Kyoto's version of a sweat lodge.

On the larger floats' rooves, experienced men called *yanegata* help keep the floats away from power lines, utility poles, and buildings. The final blocks on Shinmachi street are particularly dangerous, as the tall floats sway side to side. The men who undertake this perilous role help ensure the safety of everyone else in the festival.

*Ohayashi musicians and roof riders prepare for the July 17 procession at **Hōka Boko**.*

Tsuji Mawashi Corner Turning

The smaller yamaboko are rolled along with men pushing and pulling posts and bars at their shoulders, rather than pulling by long ropes. To turn a smaller

*Men turning **Ashikari Yama** on their shoulders. These smaller yama weigh up to 1.6 tons.*

yamaboko float, the men can hoist it higher on their shoulders to rotate it in the direction they need to go. It's a test of balance and teamwork.

The larger floats require dozens of volunteer men called *hikiko* to pull them with long, thick ropes. Men walk next to the wheels, periodically inserting wedges under them as they move to keep them going straight. When the float needs to turn along the procession route, the hikiko have to rotate each yamaboko 90 degrees. However, the floats' wheels are directionally fixed—they do not turn left and right on their axles—so the floats must be turned by other means, and without injury, death, or other damage. How is this dangerous feat accomplished? With the incredible *tsuji mawashi* corner turning. You can watch this astonishing process at the major corners on the float route (see **Maps**).

The ondotori *"conductors" help turn* **Tsuki Boko** *during* tsuji mawashi.

Men prepare **Kikusui Boko** *for* tsuji mawashi.

First, long strips of bamboo are laid out on the street and covered with water to make them slippery. Next, the hikiko pull the float onto the bamboo. Then the men use all the strength they have to simultaneously push the wheels and pull the float ropes. This is how they slide the float wheels over the wet bamboo as much as they can towards the new direction. They repeat this whole time-consuming process several times, until the float is facing 90 degrees from where it started. This extremely risky undertaking has to be seen to be believed.[38]

Men pull the ropes, push the wheels, and pry them with levers to turn **Niwatori Boko** *in* tsuji mawashi.

Tsuji mawashi allows us to clearly see and hear the importance of the *ohayashi* music and *ondotori* "conductors." Their tempo, calls, movements, and fan gestures can make the difference between a good slide and a bad one, between a relatively short turn around a corner or a tortuously long one. A complete tsuji mawashi can take up to 30 minutes for the largest floats,[39] and there are at least four corners in the procession (depending on where the float's final chōnai destination is located).

---

[38] People keen to watch tsuji mawashi make the corners of the procession some of the most crowded areas. See my YouTube channel, **The Gion Festival**, for a video of tsuji mawashi.

[39] Since Shijō, Kawaramachi, and Oike streets got widened as fire breaks during World War 2, the time required has been halved compared to when the streets on the route were narrower, one festival elder told me.

With Japan being such a small and densely populated country, some of the corners are truly tight. One festival elder told me of how, when he was a young boy, a shop on the corner had to remove all of its goods from the front of the store every year so that the float ropes could be pulled through the extra space.

The ondotori *"conductors" gesture and call out, indicating when everyone should get ready to turn* **Kankō Boko**.

The final collective tsuji mawashi takes place at the Oike-Shinmachi intersection as the Saki Matsuri procession winds down here around noon. The various floats take different routes to go back to their own neighborhoods from Shinmachi, as allowed by their size, the width of the streets, and details like electric wires. Many of the larger hoko like **Niwatori Boko** and **Kikusui Boko** still have a few tsuji mawashi to do in order to make it home.

By 14:30 on July 17, decorations on even the larger floats like **Kankō Boko**'s *are mostly gone, just a few hours after the end of the procession.*

Once the floats arrive back at their **chōnai**, the musicians dismount, and the dismantling of the float begins almost immediately. If you go for lunch and come back in a few hours, you'll be amazed at the change in scene. By the next day, most signs of the Saki Matsuri will be completely gone, not to appear again until the following year. And so we recall Japan's Buddhist philosophy of *mono-no-aware*—appreciating the fleeting beauty of this world.

Please continue reading for details on each individual float.

Abura Tenjin Yama 油天神山: The Oil Thunder-Deity Float

On Aburanokōji street, south of Ayanokōji street.

The Abura Tenjin Yama centers around a Shintō shrine containing a small statue of the thunder-god ***Tenjin***. The street the float is on, Aburanokōji, means "Oil Lane," providing the other part of the float's name.[40]

Abura Tenjin Yama's beautiful Shintō shrine atop its float. Shintō shrines always have a mirror at their center, a profound meditation.

*Some diverse antique textiles on display during **yoiyoiyama**.*

The thunder-god Tenjin started out as Sugawara no Michizane, a ninth-century court scholar, politician, and poet. Though born into a family of modest means, Sugawara was intelligent and talented, and rose unusually high at imperial court for someone of low social status. However, court intrigue led to slander and an unjust banishment from the ancient capital of Kyoto. He

---

[40] It's believed that sesame oil was produced here at some point in history.

pined away alone far away in exile for two years, before dying in disgrace.

But subsequently, the men who caused his banishment suffered a bizarre series of untimely deaths and losses, many of which involved thunderstorms. To try to transform Sugawara's *onryō* or troubled spirit into a benevolent **goryō** spirit, the emperor deified him[41] as Tenjin. Tenjin literally means "sky god," but in those days the nuance of thunder and natural disasters was strong. Since then reverence for Tenjin has morphed, and he is honored as the patron of learning; see **Arare Tenjin Yama** for more on Tenjin.

Chōnai tradition says that the statue of Tenjin in their shrine belonged to an aristocratic family that lived in this area during the Heian Era (794-1185). Thus, locals believe that Tenjin has been revered here for around a thousand years. How might that shape a community? As this connection gets passed from one generation to another, we can sense how the social fabric is woven, connecting people to one another

Abura Tenjin Yama showing off its new textiles in the July 17 procession.

---

[41] See the section on **Pleasing the Gods** for how this fits into Shintō belief.

today, to chōnai residents in the past, and to future generations as well.

The **chōnai** sets out red felt-covered benches for visitors, and they've innovated modern lighting that mimics the flickering candles of yesteryear for inside their *chōchin* paper lanterns at night. The peaceful ambiance makes this quiet neighborhood an inviting one.

Abura Tenjin Yama has some fine and diverse antique textiles in their collection, which we can see decorating the float before the procession on July 17. Nowadays most floats commission reproductions of these valuable antiques. Abura Tenjin Yama's **chōnai**, however, decided together to travel to Europe to do research and commission new textiles. Ultimately they chose new designs inspired by the Lady and the Unicorn tapestry cycle at the Cluny Museum in Paris. "The Gion Festival tradition has always been about gathering and sharing the best from around the world," one **chōnai** member explained.

Why does the **chōnai** decorate Abura Tenjin Yama with its new textiles in the July 17 procession, rather than its antique ones? This is a matter of some debate.[42] "The tradition is to put out new things, like people showing off our new clothes," he continued. "This way of thinking is important for the festival—this is how it's always been."

---

[42] See my YouTube channel, **The Gion Festival,** for a video on "The Great Gion Festival Textile Debate."

Arare Tenjin Yama 霰天神山: The Hail Thunder-God Float

On Nishiki-kōji (one block north of Shijō) street, between Muromachi and Shinmachi streets.

Arare Tenjin Yama is dedicated to the thunder deity *Tenjin-sama*, as is **Abura Tenjin Yama**. "Arare" means "hail;" **chōnai** tradition holds that during a terrible fire in 1510, hail suddenly started to fall in this neighborhood. Incredibly, the hail put out the fire, and a tiny statue of Michizane inexplicably fell on the rooftops together with the hail. This inspired the neighborhood to dedicate this float to Tenjin-sama and the miraculous fire-quenching *arare*.

The float also magically survived the Great Fires of 1788 and 1864 that destroyed so many others (such as **Kikusui Boko** around the corner). This is the place to get an amulet to protect from lightning and fire.

Spiritually eclectic: Arare Tenjin Yama features a Shintō shrine and a rare 16th-century Belgian tapestry fragment featuring pagan Greek nature spirits from The Iliad *(see also **Niwatori Boko**). On the opposite side of the float is a textile of a Chinese dragon (see **Art Treasures**). The golden zigzag* gohei *at the float's front purify the city streets.*

As introduced with **Abura Tenjin Yama**, Tenjin is the deified spirit of virtuous ninth-century scholar, poet, and statesman Sugawara no Michizane. As mentioned, in earlier centuries he was more closely related to thunder and related disasters. But due to Sugawara's excellence in learning, Japanese have come to pray to him as a god of education, asking or expressing thanks for his assistance with success in exams.

Visitors may pay respects to the statue of **Sugawara no Michizane** *inside this small shrine in Arare Tenjin Yama's* **kaisho**. *The golden zigzags are* gohei, *lacquered paper that's waved over spaces in Shintō purification rituals.*

Though exiled unjustly, history tells us that Michizane suffered with dignity and loyalty to the emperor who had banished him. For these reasons, his life represents an archetypal human experience. It's believed that praying to Tenjin may provide comfort when feeling unfairly wronged. This makes him a popular deity, with more than 12,000 Tenjin shrines estimated in Japan.

A lovely greeting at Arare Tenjin Yama.

A narrow passageway from Nishiki street opens up onto this float's **kaisho** display area, a lovely, small courtyard adjacent to its classic *kura* storehouse. Traditionally, central Kyoto is known for this urban planning configuration—a long, narrow passage opening to a courtyard and a kura. Note the exquisite artistry of the small shrine to Michizane, built in 1714.

The beautifully crafted fence around the shrine features small images of oxen: legend holds that the bull pulling Sugawara's funeral cart laid down in the road and refused to move. The ox subsequently became something like Sugawara's totem, with statues at every Tenjin shrine.

Plum blossoms, beloved by Sugawara, are another major element of Tenjin tradition. Sharing their sweet fragrance, they're the first flower to bloom after a bitter Kyoto winter. Sugawara wrote some beautiful and well-known poems about his favorite plum tree. As part of this legacy, you can see plum blossoms here at Arare Tenjin Yama, at **Abura Tenjin Yama**, and at every Tenjin shrine in the country.

Ashikari Yama 芦刈山:
The Reed Cutter: Love Reunited

On Ayanokōji street, between Nishinotōin and Aburanokōji streets.

Ashikari Yama is based on a touching **noh theater** play written by the 14th-15th century genius actor and noh playwright Zeami (pron. "Zay-ah-mi'), Japan's answer to Shakespeare. We know that Zeami attended the Gion Festival, and that noh theater used to be performed on the

Ashikari Yama: A scene from a famous noh theater play by Zeami.

Gion Festival floats before the actors were replaced with sacred statues. What a different kind of festival it must have been in those days.

The scene on Ashikari Yama features a man cutting river reeds to sell to people who made them into mats and blinds. Despite the sacred statue's beautiful (and costly) **noh** costume, this work is humble day labor.

In Zeami's play, *Ashikari (The Reed Cutter)*, the man's wife sees him for the first time after three years of separation. The couple had been too poor to support themselves, so she had sought work in Kyoto's imperial court. Meanwhile, he started cutting and selling river reeds in present-day Osaka, away from the refined culture of the ancient capital.

THE GION FESTIVAL

The float captures the mysterious beauty[43] of this poignant moment of joy mixed with sadness. The wife and husband had separated unwillingly, desperately, seeking survival and a better life. The wife travels to find her life partner once more, and is—incredibly, since this was before post offices, phones, or email—able to find him. However, she discovers him in lowly circumstances.

But their love for one another prevails.

For whatever reason, marital love is not a common theme in Japanese arts. The play *Ashikari* and the Ashikari Yama float are unusual in that this couple felt overjoyed to reunite: they moved back to Kyoto together to start their life anew. Though Ashikari Yama shows us a scene filled with heartache, it's also a story known for its happy ending.

Ashikari Yama's earliest known existence is confirmed to be 1500. In its **kaisho** display area you can see the original head used on its sacred statue. It is signed and dated "1537" by the sculptor Kō-un from the famous Kei school of sculpture, renowned for its extraordinary sculptors being

Sun and rain during the procession notwithstanding, the Gion Festival community takes good care of their treasures: This kimono is 430 years old. Contemporary textile of cranes at left.

---

[43] Zeami embraced a dramatic philosophy of *yūgen* or "mysterious beauty."

committed Buddhist practitioners as well. The kimono that originally adorned the sacred statue dates to 1589 and is in outstanding condition. Float lore says it was gifted to the float by shōgun Oda Nobunaga. It's the oldest sacred statue costume in the festival, and designated an Important Cultural Property by the Japanese government. To better conserve these treasures, neither is used, but both originals are displayed. The "new" replica statue head is a "mere" few hundred years old.

The textiles featuring a lion and cranes[44] on the front and back of the float are based on designs by internationally recognized modern artist Yamaguchi Kayo.

Ashikari Yama's comprehensive website[45] is perhaps the best bilingual one among all the Gion Festival floats.

---

[44] Curiously these are **Sarus Cranes**, not **Red-crowned Cranes**, Japan's endangered national bird.
[45] Ashikariyama.jp

Ayagasa Boko 綾傘鉾: The Damask Umbrella Float

On Ayanokōji street between Muromachi and Shinmachi streets.

Ayagasa Boko's umbrella shape recalls the Gion Festival's earliest ninth-century processions. Paintings and descriptions from that era show people carrying different kinds of halberds, banners, umbrellas, and other tall pole-type instruments. As these got bigger or more decorated, they were attached to carts with wheels.

Look closely at the celestial beings on Ayagasa Boko's silk drapery, so finely woven that they look painted—a tribute to Kyoto's kimono heritage.

Gasa means "umbrella" and *aya* is damask, a type of textile weave. *Ayanokōji* or "Little Damask Road" is the name of the street it's on, so we can start to piece together the history of the community, probably one of specialized weavers.

The textiles hanging from its two umbrellas depict celestial beings and the four seasons, the latter dyed with Kyoto's famously artistic and subtle *yūzen* technique by Living National Treasure Moriguchi Kakō. Ayagasa Boko also includes six **chigo** children in costume and painted faces as part of their procession, the only float other than **Naginata Boko** to do so.

One of Ayagasa Boko's chigo.

Ayagasa Boko is known to have existed for at least five centuries. At some times it looked something like it does now. It's also been a larger float people could ride on with a "samurai-helmet" roof topped by an umbrella. This float burned in the Great Fire of 1864, and the current float was restored in 1979, 115 years later. The **chōnai** plans to rebuild the larger float. In their small Shintō shrine courtyard **kaisho**, we can see an antique toy model, paintings and other treasures showing us the shape, size, activities, etc. of earlier floats. Such artwork is extremely valuable for research and restoration efforts.

We can study this historic painting to learn more about what Ayagasa Boko, its dancers and musicians looked like in the past.

Speaking of research, the re-introduction of Ayagasa Boko's dynamic **dance and music**—the most exciting in the entire floats procession—was partly based on a 17th-century painting of the Gion Festival on a folding screen owned by Kyoto's Buddhist Bukkyo University. Due to evidence like this painting, it's believed that the Gion Festival historically included more dance and ritual theater, as well as music. Ayagasa Boko collaborated in research and artistic development with Bukkyo University and the Mibu Rokusai Preservation Society in southern Kyoto, where the ancient style of dance was still preserved.

This particular **dance and music** style are based on nembutsu odori, a tenth-century ritual mix of beating drums, ringing bells, dancing, and Buddhist mantra chanting. Throughout history its purpose has constantly changed. It has been used to attain Buddhist salvation, ward away evil spirits and the epidemics and other illnesses they may cause, provide relief for the spirits of the dead, and to entertain. The dancers' stick-twirling was originally meant to keep away harmful spirits or energies. These are universal elements at the heart of shamanic healing over millennia and diverse traditions.

The stick-twirling helps us to focus, and focus brings deeper engagement and health.

See the **Schedule** for dance and music rehearsal dates and times during the festival.

See the auspicious rooster statue on top of Ayagasa Boko's umbrella. Besides being a courageous animal, its crowing at dawn marks the end of darkness and the beginning of a new day. The rooster holds an egg in its claw, signifying the never-ending cycle of birth, life, and death.

I had the pleasure of working with some of Ayagasa Boko's **chōnai** members at the Portland Japanese Garden's Gion Festival event in 2018. The Ayagasa Boko float and some of its treasures were featured in the exhibit. It was a historic occasion, the first time a Gion Festival float had traveled outside of Japan.

Fune Boko 船鉾: The Ship Float

On Shinmachi street, 1.5 blocks south of Shijō street.

"Fune" means ship and this ship-shaped float is much loved for its unique form. This float reveres Japan's semi-legendary, third-century Empress Jingū and refers to the remarkable voyage that Japan's oldest history texts[46] say she made to the Silla Kingdom (present-day Korean peninsula).

Fune Boko floats along downtown Kyoto streets during the July 17 procession.

Empress Jingū is a fascinating and controversial character. While her title is "Empress," in those ancient times she would have been more like a shamanic tribal leader. "Pair rule" was standard then, and she co-ruled with her male partner, Emperor Chūai, until his early death. The tale of her subsequent voyage to Silla is full of divination (one such scene is depicted at **Urade Yama**) and mystical interactions between gods and humans. The story says the gods helped her control the ocean tides, that she subjugated Silla without a battle, and returned to Japan's shores in a boat that was heavy with tribute.[47]

---

[46] The *Kojiki* (712) and *Nihon Shōki* (720).
[47] See **Ōfune Boko** and **Urade Yama** for more about Empress Jingū. **Ōfune Boko** represents the same ship as Fune Boko, on its return journey to Japan.

On returning to Japan, she gave birth to the next emperor, Ōjin, who eventually became the warrior god Hachiman, of **Hachiman Yama**. That both mother and baby survived this epic journey made her a patroness of safe pregnancy and birth, and amulets are sold here to provide this protection.

Scholars continue to debate whether Jingū was a historical or mythological person. Is she truly too fantastic to be real, or do remarkable women get erased from history's pages?

The sacred statue of Empress Jingū venerated at Fune Boko's display area gives us a taste of Japan's little-known *onna-bugeisha* culture of female martial artists.[48] Marvel at the craftsmanship of her full armor and swords.

The **chōnai** alternates between adorning Jingū's sacred statue with two traditional **noh theater** masks, one dating to the 1440s and the other to 1833. Chōnai elders enjoy speaking of how the older mask was saved from Kyoto's Great Fire of 1864: While his own home burned, the rescuer escaped with the mask to southern Kyoto and kept it with him in a bamboo forest[49] for three days and nights without food and water, until the fire passed. That's how much he valued the sacred statue's noh mask. We can sense that the

---

[48] **Urade Yama** and **Suzuka Yama** also share this culture.
[49] Live Kyoto bamboo is fire resistant.

THE GION FESTIVAL

float treasures' worth comes from more than age and artistry—people have put themselves in great danger to preserve them for future generations, currently us. We can pay it forward by supporting the Gion Festival today.

In the Fune Boko **kaisho** display area, we see statues of three additional deities, which are dated "1616." These are Shintō kami spirits who helped Jingū's journey be successful. From left to right as you face them:

Ryūjin, the dragon god of the sea;
Kashima Myōjin, a warrior god also related to safe maritime travel;
Sumiyoshi Myōjin, a guardian deity of seafaring travel.

This float is known for its inlaid mother-of-pearl rudder (made in 1793), gilded painted ceiling (1834) with 20 kinds of flowers, and nearly 3-D embroidered dragon tapestry (1837). The giant gilded bird (1761) at Fune Boko's prow is a mythical *geki*, similar to a phoenix but related to water instead of fire.

Fune Boko has been a festival leader in striking a balance between tradition and innovation. Its

Small dragon carvings around Fune Boko's exterior.

pioneering activities offer promise for both the conservation of Gion Festival traditions and their adaptation to the modern world. Read more in the **Community** section.

Across the street from Fune Boko, you can enjoy the beautiful **traditional architecture** and garden of Nagae-Ke, former home of the Nagae family, long-time supporters of Fune Boko. If conserving such places has value for you, let the staff know—Kyoto and Japanese law offer no protection at present, and relatively few of these buildings remain in Kyoto's downtown core.

HAKUGA YAMA 伯牙山:
UNDERSTANDING THROUGH SOUND

On Ayanokōji street, between Shinmachi and Nishi-notōin streets.

Hakuga Yama venerates a Chinese man named Hakuga (Bo Ya in Chinese), perhaps the best-known musician of Chinese antiquity. He was a virtuoso who played music and composed on the *qin*—a horizontal Chinese harp—in the Spring and Autumn Period (eighth-fifth centuries B.C.E.). In ancient China, literati needed to master poetry, calligraphy, the qin, and the strategic game of go. As such, the qin was a refined instrument of meditation, not a form of entertainment.

Legend has it that Hakuga (Bo Ya) destroyed his instrument when he learned that the only person who understood his music had died.

Incredibly, Bo Ya's music is still played today. But the Hakuga Yama float shows Bo Ya about to ax his *koto,* the Japanese version of a qin. Why would he destroy it?

Even though Bo Ya's mastery was widely recognized, he still felt that no one truly understood his music. But one day a humble woodcutter named Shōshiki (Chinese: Zhong Ziqi) heard Bo Ya's music from a distance. To Bo Ya's delight, Ziqi could perfectly interpret what Bo Ya was expressing. Thereafter the

Chinese phrase "to know one's sound" became synonymous with an ideal, empathic friendship that transcends differing backgrounds.

This Kyoto-made textile shows Taoist Immortals. Their intensive spiritual practices give them supernatural abilities, sometimes related to their animal familiar—such as the flying kirin *mythical beast, tiger, goose, and peacock shown here.*[50]

Ziqi died, and when Bo Ya learned this, he again felt that no one understood his music. Why play, then? He destroyed his instrument and vowed to never play again. The Hakuga Yama float portrays this heart-wrenching scene.

The sacred statue of Hakuga/Bo Ya is signed and dated "1790." Note the artistic mastery of the expression on its face, a subtle blend of passion, sadness, and anger.

There's a mystery here, though. It's said that Bo Ya only broke the *strings* of his qin instrument, not the qin itself. Hakuga Yama may be telling a different tale. In fourth-century China, a literati named Tai Andō (Chinese: Dai Kui) was so gifted on the qin that he was invited to play for the emperor. Since playing the qin was a personal meditation, not court entertainment, he refused. The emperor persisted, and Andō finally

---

[50] See **Kakkyō Yama** and **Koi Yama** for more on Taoism in the Gion Festival.

destroyed his qin—possibly at risk of his life—to make his point.[51]

One textile features a Chinese poem about stargazing, a reference to the *Tanabata* Star Festival that also takes place every July. It's an ancient tradition to play the qin and koto during the Star Festival.

Hakuga Yama is an excellent example of the influence of Chinese classics on Japanese culture, and how Kyotoites have always prided themselves in demonstrating their knowledge.

This float's treasures are displayed inside an entryway to the historic Sugimoto **private residence**, where the tenth generation of Sugimotos continues to live. As part of the festival celebrations, the family graciously opens their home to the public and displays exquisite family heirlooms. Our entry ticket fees support the preservation of this beautiful building.

Behind Hakuga Yama's koto, the blue textile includes an ancient Chinese poem celebrating an auspicious star. Tassel-holders at left are stylized moths.

---

[51] This story is from a book of essays on Kyoto living by the late Professor Sugimoto Hidetarō, who lived with Hakuga Yama for his entire life.

Hakurakuten Yama 白楽天山: Zen—Simply Profound

On Muromachi street, south of Ayanokōji street.

This float shows a moment of profound Zen teaching, likened to a thunderclap in the mind. The sacred statue in purple is the seventh-eighth century Chinese Zen master Dōrin (Chinese: Daolin). Dōrin embodied some of the "crazy wisdom" and eccentricities found in Zen. For one, he was known to sit zazen in a pine tree. Birds nested in the branches around him, and so he became known as the "Bird's Nest Zen Master." We can see him sitting in the pine tree during the July 17 procession.

Dōrin teaching Zen from his pine tree seat.

The float depicts a visit from Hakurakuten (Chinese: Bai Letian), a prolific Tang-dynasty poet famous for themes of social justice and an accessible style. He also became governor of the local district, and visited Dōrin, observing:

"What a dangerous seat you have up in the tree!"

"Yours is far worse than mine," retorted the master.

"I am the governor of this district, and I don't see what danger there is in it."

"Then, you don't know yourself! When your passions burn and your mind is unsteady, what is more dangerous than that?"

The governor then asked, "What is the teaching of Buddhism?"

The master recited this famous stanza:
> "Not to commit evils,
> But to practice all good,
> And to keep the heart pure—
> This is the teaching of the Buddhas."

[Hakurakuten], however, protested, "Any child three years old knows that."

"Any child three years old may know it, but even an old man of eighty years finds it difficult to practice it."[52]

Hakurakuten Yama shows the moment of this teaching. How did it affect Hakurakuten? He's known as an accomplished Zen practitioner and helped rebuild a monastery at the famous Buddhist caves at Longmen,[53] in China's western Henan province. He lived, meditated and wrote poetry at the monastery for the last decade of his life, finally dying there.

Look closely when you can: the details are astonishing. From an embroidered decorative panel upcycled from a mid-18th century Qing court robe.

---

[52] Translated by D.T. Suzuki in *Essays in Zen Buddhism* (Third Series), Rider & Co., 1953, p. 368.
[53] Now a UNESCO World Heritage Site.

Hakurakuten's poetry enjoyed great popularity both in China and Japan during his lifetime and was quoted in *The Tale of Genji,* Murasaki Shikibu's famous tenth-century novel. This scene of Dōrin teaching Hakurakuten has been a popular subject for many Asian painters over the centuries.

Hakurakuten Yama has continued to purchase and commission new and antique textiles, including a depiction of Beijing's Temple of Heaven, woven by the renowned textile artist Yamaga Seika in 1953.

The Gion Festival aesthetic combines diverse genres and themes put together. Note the 16th-century fragment of a Belgian tapestry on the left, showing Aeneas fleeing the fall of Troy, from Homer's Iliad. *The rest of this tapestry decorates two floats in the Otsu Festival in neighboring Shiga Prefecture. See* **Koi Yama** *for more on these unique Belgian tapestries.*

The Gion Festival is always adapting and changing, and how each float does this differently makes for a beautiful mosaic of diverse community achievements. Hakurakuten Yama has partnered with Doshisha University's Center for Japanese Language and Culture to translate their excellent website[54] into 13 languages and counting.

---

[54] https://hakurakutenyama.jp/

Hōka Boko 放下鉾: The Renunciate's Float

On Shinmachi street, north of Shijō street.

In the middle of various *hoko* floats' *shingi* "mast pole" are tiny shrines containing small statues of deities, sacred parts of the float ornamentations. It's said that Hōka Boko's figurine is a *hōkazō* or homeless monk.

Hōka Boko's ohayashi musicians playing at night before the 17 July procession.

Abandoning the common world, this particular kind of monk wandered, spreading Buddhist teachings. At times in Japanese history they used street performance as a way to share Buddhist teachings, and to receive what they needed to live. These monks were independent and could be unpredictable, even wild. Sometimes people with no spiritual realization pretended to be hōkazō just to receive money. So people were not sure about them: were they entertainers? Enlightened men sharing wisdom we ordinary people don't understand? Semi-crazed frauds? Opinions differed, and still do. There's not a lot of information about hōkazō, perhaps because they were so irregular.

When we reflect or learn more about what we're looking at, the Gion Festival reveals many mystical associations. The simple symbol atop the Hōka Boko's *shingi* "mast" represents the sun, moon, and stars. The idea is that they bring light to our world below.

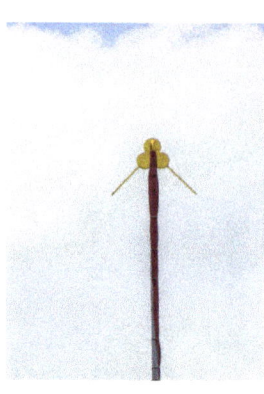

Each float's symbol atop its central pole is a unique talismanic identifier. This is Hōka Boko's.

Only the Hōka Boko and Tōrō Yama floats' statues have articulated limbs that can move. Hōka Boko's sacred doll gets manipulated to "dance" in ways very similar to **Naginata Boko's** living *chigo*-*san's* dance performance, both during the **Saki Matsuri floats procession**.

Hōka Boko records show that until 1927, it had a live chigo-san boy just as Naginata Boko does. It's also known that its current sacred doll, named Sankōmaru, began being used in 1929, though the reasons for the changeover are unknown. The high commitment and expense are likely contributors.

Hōka Boko is blessed with many diverse treasures and a fairly large space to display them in. Enjoy the beautiful crane carvings under the roof peak, and the drawings they're based on. Hōka Boko treasures' origins are well researched and displayed (with some English), which is unusual. As mentioned, the Gion Festival has long been a mostly oral tradition. Someone put a lot of effort into this for us.

As with many floats, the Hōka Boko **chōnai** believed that some of their treasures were based on designs by a particular famous artist, but there was no evidence this was true. In Hōka Boko's case, the story went that some of its antique textiles (depicting scenes in a Chinese scholar's garden) were based on paintings by the 18th-century painter and haiku poem master Yosa Buson. In 2006 an antique manuscripts dealer discovered a letter from Buson thanking Hōka Boko for their commission and confirming payment. Fortunately, they contacted Hōka Boko, and now we all know.

The Hōka Boko doll "performing" its dance. The ocean-themed textile below it is based on a famous painted scroll depicting a Buddhist shape-shifter.[56]

In addition, I shared with Hōka Boko a song I'd learned studying traditional *kyōgen* dance,[55] entitled *Hōkazō*. There's a noh theater play by the same name, but the kyōgen dance was new to them.

In such ways, the history of the Gion Festival is still alive and taking shape. What discoveries await us?

Every year the Hōka float's position in the July 17 procession is fixed, towards the end. All three floats

---

[55] I had the enormous pleasure and privilege of studying with Living National Treasure Shigeyama Sensaku IV.
[56] The scroll and textile depict a legend about Shanmiao, a woman who transformed herself into a dragon to protect Uisang, the monk she loved. Uisang was the founder of the Huayan or "Flower Garland" school of Buddhism in Korea (*Kegon* in Japan). The 750-year-old scroll, a National Treasure, belongs to the Kyoto temple Kozanji.

on Shinmachi street (the last street in the procession's route) need to be well-coordinated so that they can arrive back to where they started, without blocking one another's way. You can watch the carefully orchestrated maneuvering and astonishing ***tsuji mawashi*** corner-turning at the Oike-Shinmachi intersection, between 11:00 and noon. Expect crowds.

HOSHŌ YAMA 保昌山: COURAGEOUS LOVE

On Higashinotōin street (one block east of Karasuma), 3.5 blocks south of Shijō street.

Hoshō Yama relates to romantic love, an unusual theme for a festival float, or statuary. In ancient Japan, romance was mostly found in poems and novels written by women. But Hoshō Yama venerates an enamored 11th-century noble warrior Hoshō Hirai,[57] famed for his courage in battle.

Hoshō was also brave enough to fall in love with Izumi Shikibu, one of the five women among Japan's famed Thirty-Six Immortal Poets (see **Urade Yama**). She was a passionate woman and devout Buddhist with a colorful love life for her times, all documented in her distinguished poems. She also loved plum blossoms, and told Hoshō she would return his affections if he brought her some plum blossoms from—of all places—an imperial palace garden. If caught, the penalty would have been death. So we can see on the float that Hoshō is wearing full armor. He's also escaping with quite a lot of plum blossoms in hand,

The things we do for love. Note court badges at bottom of image.

---

[57] He is better known to history as Fujiwara no Yasumasa.

showing the combination of his courage and great love for Shikibu. Amulets are sold here for strengthening romantic bonds.

The head of the sacred statue of Hoshō is nearly 600 years old, and, together with the float's intriguing antique textiles, famously survived The Great Tenmei Fire of 1788, which devastated the surrounding area.

Men and tigers walk on water in one of Hoshō Yama's intriguing paintings and textiles.

I once saw a fire drill at Hoshō Yama, and the fireman practiced leaving the building with a head-sized box marked "Important Cultural Property."

The large embroidered textiles that decorate three sides of the float are based on intriguing paintings by the remarkable 18th-century artistic genius **Maruyama Ōkyo**. Hoshō Yama is unusual in that they have the original Maruyama paintings (now on folding screens), the original embroidered textiles completed in 1772, as well as contemporary reproductions.

Float patrons say the scenes show a second-century Chinese explorer and diplomat named Chōken (Chinese: Zhang Qian), considered the father of the Silk Road. Look closely and see how some of the characters are with their animal familiars, sometimes walking on water, or holding objects emitting mysterious vapors. These magical pictures refer to Zhang Qian's semi-legendary exploits.

Similar original designs for other Japanese-made textiles and metalwork in the festival may still exist. Perhaps they are awaiting discovery and a reunion with the Gion Festival (read about a similar find at **Hōka Boko**). Unfortunately, public display space is limited at every float, so you're unlikely to see the original paintings or textiles. The modern replicas cost around US$150,000 each, to give you a general idea of these treasures' worth. In addition, here we can see a row of 17th-century embroidered Chinese court badges upcycled into a decorative textile panel (see also **Kakkyō Yama**).

Hoshō Yama is located in a two-story traditional Kyoto **kyōmachiya** townhouse, an excellent example of traditional architecture in the festival. From the second story, the sacred statue of Hoshō can radiate good romantic karma on visitors and passersby. Local residents get together to make all of the float's plum flowers by hand with handmade *washi* Japanese paper.

Iwatō Yama 岩戸山: The Stone Door Float

On Shinmachi street, south of Bukkōji (2.5 blocks south of Shijō) street.

Iwatō Yama venerates three major deities from Japanese history and mythology. Their remarkable tales come from the eighth-century *Kojiki* and *Nihon Shoki*, Japan's two oldest texts about its earliest history and culture. Interestingly, Iwatō Yama relates to three important but separate myths in earliest Japanese history.

Izanagi and friends on the roof of Iwatō Yama. Courageous men ride on float roofs to help navigate utility wires and other obstacles.

The primordial male Japanese deity Izanagi-no-Mikoto is Iwatō Yama's first sacred statue, and the only one in the entire Gion Festival to ride on a float roof. According to myth, he and his female partner Izanami-no-Mikoto co-created the Japanese islands, various gods, and the Japanese people.

However, he birthed some of the most important Shintō deities all by himself. The *Kojiki* tells us that Izanagi washed his left eye, and from that, the sun goddess Amaterasu Ōmikami was born. This was part

Lighting Up the Heavens

Amaterasu is the second deity revered at Iwatō Yama. She is best known as Japan's sun goddess. Legend tells us that all of Japan's emperors descend from her. The name *Iwatō Yama* means "stone door float." In one myth, Amaterasu became terribly angry with her younger brother and god of storms **Susano-o-no-Mikoto**,[59] the central deity of the Gion Festival and **Yasaka Shrine**. Enraged, she ran inside a cave and blocked its opening with a large boulder—the stone door. Since she is the sun goddess, that meant darkness for everyone and everything on the planet. What then?

The other gods wept, cried, and schemed, hoping to lure Amaterasu back out of the cave. No success. Finally, the goddess Ama-no-Uzeme did such a wild striptease that all the other gods roared with laughter.

---

[58] Additionally, Tsukiyomi the moon god (revered at **Tsuki Boko**) was born from Izanagi's right eye as he washed it, and the god of storms and the Gion Festival **Susano-o-no-Mikoto** was born from Izanagi's nose. *The Kojiki*, pp. 50-51. This story calls to mind how the Greek goddess Athena was born from Zeus's head, or how the Buddhist deity White Tara was born from Kannon's tears of compassion.

[59] According to the *Kojiki*, he threw a dead horse on some of Amaterasu's attendants, injuring some and killing others (pp. 63-64).

Amaterasu opened the stone door just enough to see what was going on.

Wood carving of Susano-o-no-Mikoto and gilt sparrows below Iwatō Yama's roof peak.

The god Tajikara-no-Mikoto, known for his great physical strength, threw the giant stone far away so that Amaterasu and her sunlight had to come back out. He is the third deity venerated at Iwatō Yama, for literally saving the day.

An elder at Iwatō Yama told me that in past centuries, the **chōnai** would decide each year whether to adorn its float with one deity, or another, or two or three together. Now it's fixed at all three.

The third myth that Iwatō Yama celebrates is that of **Susano-o-no-Mikoto's** victory over Yamata no Orochi, an eight-headed dragon. A beautiful wooden carving of Susano-o graces one roof peak, while a carving of the dragon decorates the opposite peak.

Note the beautiful Momoyama school gilt paintings of flowers and sparrows underneath the roof, dating to around 1920. There are no artisans skilled at this type of painting at present. So Iwatō Yama is working with the government Agency for Cultural Affairs about how to restore them.[60]

---

[60] Cities like Firenze have become known for both art and restoration. Could the Gion Festival be a wellspring for Kyoto to become a world-class center for restoration?

THE GION FESTIVAL

An intriguing feature of Iwatō Yama is that its sacred statue of Amaterasu depicts her as a male. This is a good example of Japan's long and diverse history of gender flexibility.

Iwatō Yama is a *hiki-yama*, or "pulled yama." It gets pulled, like a hoko. But note that its central mast pole remains a pine tree, like other yama.

Iwatō Yama in the July 17 procession.

Kakkyō Yama 郭巨山: Confucian and Taoist Teachings

On Shijō street, between Shinmachi and Nishinotōin streets. The float is on the north side of the street, and its treasures are on the south side.

Kakkyō Yama tells a third-century Chinese story of family allegiance and respect for one's elders, a central theme in Confucian teachings.[61] In many world cultures, an elderly person is the living vehicle of decades of experience and resulting wisdom. As a result, Confucianism considers elders more valuable than less experienced youth.

Kakkyō and his son celebrate after finding a pot of gold. Kakkyō Yama is the only small yama with a roof. Note court badges framing the textile (see below).

Kakkyō (Guo Ju in Chinese) was a poor man whose family was suffering from severe hunger. His ill, elderly mother would give the little food she had to his infant son, making herself weaker. Heartsick, he and his wife decided to sacrifice their son's life, so that there would be more food for his elderly

---

[61] A popular 13th-14th-century Chinese text, *The Twenty-Four Paragons of Filial Piety*, taught Confucian values through Kakkyō's story and 23 others.

mother. They reasoned that they could have another child, but not another mother.

He started digging a grave to bury his son. As he dug, he hit something hard: a pot of gold, with his name on it. It was a reward for his devotion to the woman who had given him life and raised him. Is it a metaphor?

Kakkyō's grave still exists as part of The Dutiful Son Temple, a pilgrimage site in China's Shandong province. On Kakkyō Yama we see sacred statues of Kakkyō and his son (sculpted in 1789), celebrating their problem resolved.

This textile shows Taoist Immortal Li Tueguai sending his soul via a vapor cloud as other Taoist Immortals look on.

Kakkyō Yama has some fascinating Japanese embroidered textiles depicting Taoists' mystical powers, based on paintings by Ishida Yūtei and Maruyama Ōshin (teacher and grandson of Maruyama Ōkyo, respectively), from the 18th century. With similar textiles at **Hakuga Yama** and **Tokusa Yama**, we can surmise that Taoism was popular among Gion Festival patrons around that time.[62] Each textile shows us some of the Taoist Immortals and their respective mystical powers, cultivated through many years of spiritual practice. The items they hold, or what they

---

[62] Also see **Koi Yama** regarding Taoism in the Gion Festival.

are doing, give us clues about which Taoist Immortal they are, and what they are known for.

More recently the float's **chōnai** commissioned striking contemporary tapestries illustrating the four seasons, adapted from famous 20th-century paintings by Uemura Shōkō. New works like these stimulate Kyoto's world-famous weaving and dyeing industries.

Kakkyō Yama has good information available about its float and its treasures in several languages, including mention of a visit by renowned Japanese culture scholar Ernest Fenollosa[63] in 1888.

This beautifully painted chikakushi *panel also helps hang the textiles on Kakkyō Yama. Above it is a lacquered railing with metalwork leaves. Below it are embroidered Chinese court badges.*

Note the golden embroidered squares with animal symbols lining the antique textile that decorates the front of the float on alternating years. These are 17th-century Chinese court badges. Ming[64] imperial court officials wore them on their robes to identify their role and status. Gion Festival patrons cleverly had them sewn together to decorate their float.[65]

---

[63] Fenollosa's collection of Japanese art is now at Boston's Museum of Fine Arts, where he was head of the Oriental Art department.
[64] The Ming Dynasty lasted from 1368 until 1644.
[65] We can see more of these Ming Court badges made into float decorations at **Ashikari Yama** and **Hoshō Yama**.

Kankō Boko 函谷鉾: The Valley Pass Float

On the north side of Shijō street, just west of Karasuma street.

By tradition, Kankō Boko is always the second **hoko** in the procession, after **Naginata Boko**. With this arrangement, Kankō Boko's **chōnai** members embrace the progressive attitudes of a family's second son, compared to Naginata Boko's more orthodox upholding of tradition.

The July 17 procession, with Kankō Boko's ohayashi *musicians and sacred doll, named* Katamaru, *carved in 1840.*

The clearest example of this is Kankō Boko's outspoken support of **women** in the Gion Festival. Officially the festival is men-only and has been for at least the last 350 years. In 1947, Kankō Boko was the first float to allow women visitors to board it during the days before the July 17 procession. This was perhaps the first time women had been on a Gion Festival float since the early Edo Period. Its **ohayashi music** troupe has

Kankō Boko's ohayashi *music troupe members take a break.*

openly allowed girls and women for the last two decades.

Since 2017 Kankō Boko's **chōnai** members have been experimenting with 360° video. In this way, people can experience various festival activities up close and personal, as chōnai members do.

China's Famous Kankō (Han Gu) Pass

Kankō is the Japanese name for the famously strategic Han Gu Pass, on the border of China's Shanxi and Henan Provinces. Han Gu means "Valley." Just outside of the ancient capital of Xi'an, it was a crucial fortification in the Great Wall of China.

The float name comes from a unique historical episode. During the Warring States Period (475-221 B.C.E.), Lord Meng Chang of Qi and his men were in a life-or-death situation in Han Gu. They needed to escape through the pass in the middle of the night.

Contemporaries admired Lord Chang for welcoming all kinds of people, and recognizing talent where others did not. He had taken under his protection a man whose talent was to perfectly imitate any sound. With lives at stake, the man mimicked the sound of a cock crowing. He did it so well that the men guarding the pass

Artistic glories under Kankō Boko's roof peak. Note the gilt paintings of chickens.

THE GION FESTIVAL

believed it was dawn. They opened the gate and unknowingly set free their enemies.

A small statue of Lord Chang is revered inside the tiny shrine halfway up Kankō Boko's *shingi* mast pole.

Until recently much of the Gion Festival floats' history and culture has been passed by word of mouth. There are many opportunities for further research and discoveries. Why the Kankō Boko community originally chose this tale for their float's theme, for example, is currently unclear.

Meanwhile, the Han Gu Pass is also celebrated as the birthplace of Taoism. According to Taoist legend, Lao Tzu decided to write the *Tao Te Ching* while traveling through the pass gate, and he wrote it in Han Gu. While numerous other floats' textile hangings show Taoist scenes,[66] there are no known Taoist connections with the Kankō Boko float.

To give an idea of ongoing festival requirements, in 2007 Kankō Boko replaced one of their float's main two timbers, which they'd used for 150 years. It took a decade and US$50,000 to locate and prepare its replacement, a 300-year old wild cherry tree from westernmost Japan.

Kankō Boko has some rare and outstanding textiles in their collection from Japan, India, Korea, China, and Europe, including a rare 17th-century **textile** from Lahore in excellent condition. But they may be most proud of their large 16th-century Belgian

---

[66] See **Hakuga Yama**, **Hoshō Yama**, **Kakkyō Yama**, **Tokusa Yama**, and **Koi Yama** for more on Taoism in the Gion Festival.

tapestry, an Important Cultural Property.⁶⁷ You can see the original and a recent reproduction in their kaisho space, one of the few places where we can see both side by side. You can decide for yourself whether you favor new commissions, purchase of antiques, or commissioned reproductions.⁶⁸

The Belgian tapestry shows Rebekah giving water to Isaac, a scene from the Old Testament's Book of Genesis.

---

[67] Different from other Belgian tapestries in the Gion Festival (see **Koi Yama**), this textile came into Japan in the early 1600s via the Dutch East India Company's trade concession in Nagasaki. It appeared on Kankō Boko in the 1700s, according to Kankō Boko records. How the textile got from Nagasaki to the Gion Festival is still unknown.
[68] See my YouTube channel, *The Gion Festival*, for a video on this topic.

Kikusui Boko 菊水鉾: The Chrysanthemum Water Float

On Muromachi street, one block west of Karasuma, just north of Shijō street.

"Kikusui" means "Chrysanthemum water" and refers to an ancient Chinese legend and Japanese **noh theater** play named Kiku Jidō, meaning "Chrysanthemum Boy." The story is about a 700-year-old boy who had gained eternal youth. How did he do it? By writing prayers from the Lotus Sutra on chrysanthemum leaves, and then drinking the dew. The prayer goes something like this: "Use every virtue as a tool: with a compassionate eye regard all living beings." According to the play and legend, living in this way grants long life and prosperity. The dedication it took to copy out the prayer in such a small space gave the dew magical properties.

Note Kikusui Boko's unusual "samurai helmet" roof, modern textiles, and the uncommon costumes of its ondotori *"conductors."*

The float's sacred doll is Kiku Jidō, the Chrysanthemum Boy, dressed as an actor playing the role in the noh play. We can see the chrysanthemum emblem all around this float: for one, look at the metal openwork symbol at the very top of its central *shingi* pole. There are chrysanthemums on the hubs of the float's gigantic wheels, and stylized ones on the **chōnai** members' cotton *yukata* kimono.

In the early 16th century a monk and student of Sen no Rikyū—creator of the contemporary tea ceremony—built a small tea hut at the site of this float. He loved the sweet water that came from a well that used to be here. He named it "Kikusui Well" after the legend and noh play, and the float's name came from this well. Later a noh theater was built on this site, and it was here until the mid-1990s. The float's treasures were displayed inside the theater.

Japanese tea ceremony at Kikusui Boko. The scroll on the wall dates to 1820, and shows Kikusui Boko at that time.

This float's neighborhood has had ties to the tea ceremony ever since that tea hut was here more than 400 years ago. For 2000 yen you can refresh yourself from the festival heat and humidity with matcha tea (a.k.a. "Japanese espresso") and a tea sweet. As bonuses, you can enjoy watching tea ceremony and view some of the float's treasures in an air-conditioned setting, and receive a chrysanthemum-shaped ceramic dish as a souvenir. Tea masters and their students come from all around Kyoto to help prepare and serve the tea.

Kyoto's Great Genji Fire of 1864 destroyed Kikusui Boko and numerous other Gion Festival floats. Some of its textiles were saved, however. Although the **chōnai** are rivals with one another, they support one other too:

the Kikusui Boko chōnai gifted their surviving textiles to **Yamabushi Yama**, where we can still enjoy them.

Wealthy textile merchant Matsumoto Motoharu lived in the Kikusui neighborhood, and worked with the chōnai to rebuild their float in 1952 as an expression of gratitude for his business success. We can imagine the hopefulness this must have inspired during Japan's challenging post-war era. Because the new float needed music and musicians, half of neighboring **Tsuki Boko**'s ohayashi **music** troupe moved over to Kikusui Boko.

A contemporary textile showing peacocks and flowers, by Minagawa Gekka, as Kikusui Boko prepares for the July 17 procession.

Kikusui Boko's modern decorations represent some of the best Japanese artists and craftspeople working from 1950-1990. These include the innovative Minagawa Gekka, Japan's most famous 20th-century textile artist, who created the three large textiles showing lion dogs, flying cranes, and peacocks. He also painted the powerful dragon amidst clouds that covers the ceiling on board the float. He took the high craft of traditional kimono dyeing techniques and innovated by combining various methods in new ways. This helped kimono dyeing to become recognized internationally as a sophisticated art form.

MŌSŌ YAMA 孟宗山: CONFUCIAN TEACHINGS ON FAMILY

On the west side of Karasuma street, just north of Shijō street.

Mōsō (Chinese: Meng Zong) was a lower-level government official who lived in the third century, according to a 13th-14th century Chinese text on Confucian values. His father had died when he was a boy, and his mother was seriously ill.

Note the quality of the Chinese-style costume and the many metalwork bird species adorning the black lacquered railing.

While unwell, she missed her favorite food: young bamboo shoots. But it was in the middle of a very cold and snowy winter, and bamboo shoots don't grow until spring. Longing to give his mother some relief, Mōsō searched for bamboo shoots anyway, with no success. Finally, exhausted and disheartened from his failed search, he collapsed on the ground.

Thinking of the woman who cared for him his whole life dying at home, tears flowed down Mōsō's cheeks. Where they fell on the ground, miraculously, he found some bamboo shoots, completely out of season. He cooked them up for his mother, and—amazingly—she quickly recovered her health.

THE GION FESTIVAL

The story goes that everyone agreed the miracle was made possible by Mōsō's virtuous devotion to his mother, honoring all that she'd done to raise him. We can see here the influence that Confucian values had on Kyoto culture. See **Kakkyō Yama** for more on this theme.

Enter this float's treasure display area through a narrow walkway, opening onto a lovely small courtyard lined with bamboo on one side and the float's treasures on the other. Note the fireproof *kura* storehouse in the back. This type of festival display area tends to be cooler and quieter, even when the day is hot and the festival is crowded.

Mōsō Yama's black and white bamboo: is it a painting? Or a weaving?

It's believed the sacred statue of Mōsō was carved in 1796 by the great Buddhist teacher and sculptor Kōchō, who also carved the statues on either side of the entrance gate to **Yasaka Shrine**. Note the finely executed expression on Mōsō's face. He's on his way back to his mother, carrying a bamboo shoot in his right hand, smiling at the thought of giving it to her.

The lacquered railings and *torii* gate are noted for their beautifully ornate metalwork. The railings feature 15 different species of birds, based on designs by late

19th-century artist Kōno Bairei.[69] A dramatic black-and-white picture of bamboo bending in the wind is strikingly monochrome in this colorful festival. The 1940 original is a Japanese ink painting on white silk by Kōno's best student Takeuchi Seihō. Takeuchi is famous for combining traditional Japanese aesthetics with European realism at the turn of the 20th century.

Mōsō Yama's chōchin *lanterns and a painting of geiko-san meet in the window of the art gallery next door.*

One story holds that the art gallery next door to Mōsō Yama helped arrange this work. In 2014 it was reproduced as a textile that looks like a painting, showing the skill of Kyoto's weaving traditions. You can also see Chinese embroidered tapestries upcycled from Ming (1368-1644) court robes, Japanese tapestries depicting Taoist Immortals,[70] and 17th-century Chinese embroidered phoenixes with peonies.

---

[69] Bairei also created a *Picture Album of One Hundred Birds* now in the collection of New York's Metropolitan Museum of Art.

[70] Look closely at tapestries: if they are flying in the sky, accompanied by tigers or three-legged toads, etc., such clues tell us that these are not ordinary humans.

Naginata Boko 長刀鉾: The Long Sword Float

On the north side of Shijō street, east of Karasuma street.

By tradition Naginata Boko is the first float in the **Saki Matsuri**'s annual procession on July 17. Its live *chigo* (see below) officially begins the procession with a rope-cutting ceremony. This opens the **festival gods'** sacred space for the floats to enter.

Legendary tenth-century swordsmith Sanjō Munechika crafted the original *naginata* "longsword" on top of its central *shingi* pole. Some say it possesses mystical properties and healing powers, which it showers upon the streets of Kyoto during the Gion Festival, battling harmful spirits or cutting through negative energy. The noh play *Kokiji* is about Munechika and his magical swordmaking.

*We can easily recognize Naginata Boko by its distinctive longsword (*naginata*) atop the central* shingi *pole.*

The *Chigo*, Vestige of Child Mediums

The literal translation of chigo is "immature child," indicating purity. Historically the chigo would have served as a kind of shamanic medium for divine energies called upon during the festival. Though originally all the hoko floats had an actual boy in the role of chigo, most switched to a sacred doll in the late 1800s or early 1900s. Naginata Boko's chigo is the only one that still rides on a float.[71]

Being chosen as Naginata Boko's chigo or one of his two attendants is a great honor for a Kyoto family. It's also a significant commitment. Traditionally chigo were prepared with rigorous purification rituals for the month before the festival, including not walking on the ground, not having contact with women, and eating specific foods.

Naginata Boko's chigo performs a unique traditional dance during the July 17 procession.

Today's preparations are more relaxed, but the chigo is still at the center of numerous formal rituals and ceremonies throughout the month of July. Among other things, the young boys must learn how to act in these, how to wear the special costumes, how to do a specialized dance for the **Saki Matsuri floats procession**, and how to formally open the Gion Festival procession on July 17 by cutting a sacred rope with a real sword.

---

[71] **Ayagasa Boko** has six chigo that walk with its float, and **Yasaka Shrine** has two **chigo** who ride horses.

THE GION FESTIVAL

From the afternoon of July 13 through July 16, you can purchase a souvenir at Naginata Boko (expect long lines) to view some of its remarkable treasures on the second story of its **kaisho** meeting place. This is one of the festival's more spacious display areas, with good explanations in Japanese.

In general, we can best appreciate festival art treasures by examining their details. See how the metal tassel-mounts on display so accurately represent different insects (can you name them?), for example. Or marvel at the chigo's kimono, finely handwoven by Kyoto's best weavers before modern Jacquard looms existed.[72] Note the Asian constellations—differently configured than Western ones—on the float ceilings. It is believed that geomantic symbols on earth reflected their counterparts in the heavens. One of the constellations, for example, is the Blue Dragon in the East, the same as the blue **dragon** believed to reside beneath **Yasaka Shrine** in eastern Kyoto.

This dragon-fish adorns the peak of Naginata Boko's roof.

Kyoto's kimono merchants have long prided themselves in this kind of cultural sophistication, rivaling that of the ancient capital's aristocrats.

---

[72] See also the **textile** section for information on a rare weaving in Naginata Boko's collection.

Naginata Boko is one of three floats that only allow men and boys to board—just 50 years ago, this was the norm. Before you form an opinion, appreciate that they are in the delicate position of being modern people conserving the traditions of their fathers and grandfathers in a sacred, ancient ritual. They're keenly aware of how times are changing, so it will be interesting to see how things unfold.

I had the pleasure of sharing information about Naginata Boko at a Gion Festival event at the Portland Japanese Garden in 2018, with about 25 members of their **ohayashi** musical troupe. They also played at the Boston Museum of Arts in 2014. So while Naginata Boko maintains a very traditional approach, at the same time it could be considered the most international float in the festival.

Naginata Boko's ondotori "conductors" wear haori jackets decorated with a moth pattern, showcasing Kyoto's outstanding tradition of design.

Niwatori Boko 鶏鉾: Dedicated to Peace

On Muromachi street (one block west of Karasuma street), south of Shijō street.

In ancient China, before 2000 B.C.E., the semi-legendary sage-king Emperor Yao ordered a large drum placed in the center of his capital. He instructed the people to beat the drum when they had a complaint, and promised to meet them to hear it. His reign was so tranquil that eventually chickens nested inside the drum, making chickens a symbol of widespread peace.

Niwatori Boko waiting for the July 17 procession to begin. **Ayagasa Boko** *waits to the left.*

Niwatori means "chicken" in Japanese,[73] and this float celebrates that peacefulness. An elder at Niwatori Boko (104 years old at the time of writing) told me that his dream was for the Gion Festival to be an instrument for world peace.

A model of wisdom and other virtues, Emperor Yao greatly inspired later Confucian and neo-Confucian philosopher-scholars. Again we can see the influence that Chinese culture and Confucianism had upon

---

[73] It's worth noting that the word *niwatori* sounds more beautiful than "chicken;" it literally translates to "garden bird."

Kyoto townspeople, particularly on kimono merchants. As mentioned, merchants were at the bottom of Japan's social hierarchy. Showing off sophisticated art, philosophical knowledge, and international connections through the Gion Festival provided a way for them to display and enjoy the power that they still had.

And living in the Gion Festival chōnai was an exclusive privilege. At times they were gated communities. A 1596 document of Niwatori Boko chōnai regulations outlines, among other things, undesirables: samurai might invite fighting, and farmers and entertainers were vulnerable to economic ups and downs.

Dazzling to the eye, Niwatori Boko's ohayashi troupe plays *gionbayashi* **music** *during the July 17 procession.*

Next door to this float is Ikenobo Junior College, affiliated with the historic Ikenobo, Japan's oldest and largest *ikebana* flower-arranging school. Ikenobo originated at nearby Rokkaku-dō Temple by the late 15th century; ikebana and the Gion Festival have surely been influencing each other culturally all that time. Though the Gion Festival is officially all-male, many young women from Ikenobo Junior College claim Niwatori Boko as their own, making for a colorful **chōnai** (see **hikizome**).

Notice the several layers of Niwatori Boko's *mizuhiki,* the strips of horizontal tapestries that go around all four sides of Niwatori Boko, above and below where the ohayashi **music** troupe sits. This float's mizuhiki are based on designs from Kyoto's famous Maruyama-Shijō school of painting. The famous 18th-century painter Maruyama Ōkyo[74] and his students worked from a studio located here on Shijō street, the major street Niwatori Boko faces.

See the image of the ohayashi music troupe above. The top mizuhiki is based on a design by Maruyama's student Matsumura Goshun. The second (red) mizuhiki with embroidered butterflies is based on a design by his half-brother and student Matsumura Keibun (who also painted the birds on **Naginata Boko**'s ceiling). The third mizuhiki—baskets of ikebana flowers—are believed to be based on a design by Maruyama Ōkyo himself.

Closeup of metalwork of cranes against clouds, and a mizuhiki textile depicting scenes from the Tang Imperial Court. The latter is based on a design by Matsumura Goshun, a leading follower of both Yosa Buson[75] and Maruyama Ōkyo.

---

[74] See **Hoshō Yama** and **Tsuki Boko** for more work by Maruyama Ōkyo.
[75] See **Hōka Boko** for more on Yosa Buson.

Niwatori Boko's 16th-century Belgian tapestry is an Important Cultural Property. Tapestries of this era, quality, and condition are rare even in Europe. How did these textiles end up in the Gion Festival? See **Koi Yama**, whose **chōnai** did some excellent research. Niwatori Boko's tapestry (you have to see it with your own eyes) shows a scene from the Greek classic *The Iliad*, when Troy's greatest warrior, Prince Hector, parted with his wife and son for the last time, never to meet again. Float records show that the tapestry was purchased in 1815 for 200 ryō. One gold ryō weighed about 15 grams and bought enough rice to feed a person for a year.

Shijō Kasa Boko 四条傘鉾: An Umbrella and Children's Dance

On the north side of Shijō street, between Nishinotōin and Aburakōji streets.

After a decade of preparation, local residents reintroduced Shijō Kasa Boko to the festival in 1985. This ended a 117-year absence from the Gion Festival. It's a great testament to the spirit of downtown Kyoto residents and businesses when this happens. It involves modern neighborhood residents like you and me undertaking a year-round, lifelong commitment.

Kyoto residents traditionally enjoyed Shijō Kasa Boko and other floats like this, from their second-story windows.

Kasa means "umbrella," and Shijō is the major street that this float is located on. Like **Ayagasa[76] Boko**, Shijō Kasa Boko consists of a giant umbrella on a wheeled cart. It shows us what many of the Gion Festival floats may have looked like a thousand years ago. On top of its umbrella is a young pine tree and red *gohei* sacred paper wands, used by Shintō priests in rituals to purify a space. The *gohei* on top of Shijō Kasa Boko and other floats are designed

---

[76] *Kasa* becomes *gasa*—both meaning "umbrella"—when combined with another syllable.

to purify the Kyoto streets and people in the July 17 procession.

The highlight of the Shijō Kasa Boko is its children's dance and music, unique in the festival processions. Two boys wearing costumes and *shaguma* "bear wigs" twirl long poles as part of their dance. Six more boys accompany them with bells, drums, and clave sticks. An ohayashi **music** troupe of adult men supports them with *gionbayashi* music.

Shijō Kasa Boko's bō-furi *or "wand-swinging" dance. In ancient times people believed that shaking the ritual stick could drive away harmful spirits.*

This float's history has an unresolved mystery. We know it existed before the Ōnin War began in 1467, and that it also participated in the Gion Festival in subsequent centuries. We know that the Great Genji Fire of 1864 destroyed many floats, but Shijō Kasa Boko survived, and participated in the Gion Festival until 1871. However, it disappeared in 1872.

The **chōnai**, Kyoto City, Kyoto Prefecture, and the national government's Agency for Cultural Affairs have all investigated, but still, no one knows why it suddenly vanished. One exciting thing about the Gion Festival is how many mysteries like this are waiting to be solved. As people's interest grows, new evidence and facts continue to come to light.

So when the Shijō Kasa Boko community decided to revive the float, they needed to investigate to make it authentic. They spent years researching historic documents and artwork to understand details of what the float, dance, and costumes had been like.

Over the centuries, the Gion Festival inspired various other festivals, floats, dances, and music across Japan. Sometimes cultural elements have disappeared from the Gion Festival but still exist elsewhere.

Research by the Shijō Kasa Boko **chōnai** found that in the 16th-century Shijō Kasa Boko featured a dance called *furyū odori,* which literally means "elegant dance." They also discovered that a shrine dance in neighboring Shiga Prefecture is closely related to the historical Shijō Kasa Boko dance. Called *kenketo,* this dance was popular in Kyoto in the Muromachi Era (1337-1573). The community used findings about *furyū odori* and this *kenketo* shrine dance to revive its own in 1988.

Year by year newly participating **chōnai** like this one add finely crafted items like metalwork decorations to build up the splendor of their floats.

Boys preparing for the "elegant dance" in the July 17 procession.

Enjoy Shijō Kasa Boko's dance and music rehearsals in the evenings of July 14-16. Check the **Schedule**, and confirm in person at Shijō Kasa Boko.

Taishi Yama 太子山: Japan's Saintly Genius

On Aburanokōji street, south of Bukkōji street.

Taishi Yama features Shōtoku Taishi, a sixth-century Japanese genius and statesman revered as a Buddhist saint. Among other things, he introduced Buddhism as Japan's state religion, drafted Japan's first constitution, and first centralized the government, based on influences from the Asian continent. *Taishi* means "Crown Prince."

An outstanding scholar and devout Buddhist practitioner, he commissioned the construction of numerous Buddhist temples, some of Japan's earliest. The float depicts him chopping down a cedar tree himself to build Shitennōji temple, a collaboration with expert Korean builders, in present-day Osaka. Dedicated to the divine guardian kings of the four directions, the 593 C.E. temple grounds included a hospital and pharmacy to tend to the welfare of the general population. This was a great social innovation, as previous temples had been private.

Taishi Yama shows Shōtoku Taishi chopping down a cedar tree to build one of Japan's first Buddhist temples.

THE GION FESTIVAL

A highlight of Taishi Yama is viewing Hata Ke,[77] the historic Hata family's magnificent **kyōmachiya** townhouse. Two years out of three its front rooms are used to display the Taishi Yama treasures.[78] This building was constructed in 1869 after its predecessor burned down in 1864's Great Genji Fire. Hospitable benches and umbrellas give us a chance to relax and enjoy the traditional features of Hata Ke's facade.

Each float's treasure display area is actually a shrine to the deity represented by the sacred statue.

Ancient texts tell us that one of Shōtoku Taishi's close advisors was the leader of a large clan named Hata, who came from the Paekche Kingdom, now South Korea. The contemporary Hatas have always had a close connection to Shōtoku Taishi, but only trace their family history back some 450 years, all at this location. The Chinese character for their name, "Hata," means "from the continent."

The display area facing the street is where the family business originally operated. Here we can pay respects to the sacred statue of Shōtoku Taishi and a smaller statue of Nyōirin Kannon. This form of the Buddhist bodhisattva of compassion holds a small wish-fulfilling

---

[77] http://www.hata-ke.jp/about/
[78] To visit a traditional private home and see more of its interior, see **Hakuga Yama** and **Fune Boko**.

gem and the eight-spoked[79] wheel of Buddhist teachings. As display space is limited, treasures are alternated over the years, and the textiles being shown and aired on the floats may be changed during the week too. You may see Taishi Yama's stunning 18th-century Mughal Indian golden embroidered tapestries (see the **Treasure Viewing** section), recently supplemented by vibrant, newly embroidered ones from Vietnam. See also the exquisite golden dragon metal fixtures.

These striking metalwork dragons hold decorative tassels at the corners of Taishi Yama.

To conservationists' dismay, we can also enjoy some of this float's antique textiles outdoors. Some of the **chōnai** neighborhoods believe in using the festival treasures as festival patrons have for centuries, sharing them as float decorations rather than conserving them indoors or out of sight.[80]

Note the antique tea caddy dating to the Edo Period (1603-1868). Matcha tea was offered to the festival deities, then ritually prepared and served during the July 17 procession to festival patrons: a true tea ceremony ritual. The tea caddy still accompanies Taishi Yama as part of the Gion Festival procession.

---

[79] Each spoke represents one branch of Buddhism's Eightfold Ennobling Path.

[80] See my YouTube channel, *The Gion Festival*, for a video on "The Great Gion Festival Textile Debate."

Tokusa Yama 木賊山: Father and Son Reunited

On Bukkōji street, between Nishinotōin and Aburanokōji streets.

The horsetail cutter. Note the horsetails—believed to be among the oldest plants on earth—around the float's border and in his hand.

Tokusa Yama features the central figure from a noh theater play and chant, "Tokusa," by the 14th-century genius Japanese playwright and philosopher Zeami. Noh theater is magical, but as with Shakespeare, it's much more enjoyable when you're familiar with the story and its themes. *Tokusa* is the Japanese word for the horsetail plant. The central character cuts horsetails for a living to make scouring brushes.

This play was in turn based on a classical Japanese poem from the late Heian Period (794-1185). The poem describes a scene: Cutting horsetail, between the trees on the mountain, the bright harvest moon rises. It features a play on words: the moon looks polished, and horsetail reeds are used to clean. It refers to classic

Zen Buddhism teachings about polishing our hearts and minds so they become bright and clear like the full moon, a symbol for spiritual enlightenment. Many of the treasures we see in the Gion Festival have these layers upon layers of meaning.

The noh play opens with a group of horsetail cutters, gathering *tokusa* and sharing poems (including the one above) related to their trade. The main character vows to polish his own heart and mind so that he may become enlightened.

This decorative metalwork rabbit is framed by tokusa plants.

The horsetail cutters meet a group of Buddhist monks, and the main character offers the monks food and a place to stay. He tells the monks that he had a son, who had disappeared years before. The son loved to dance and sing Zen songs, and the memory inspires the horsetail cutter to dance himself. Then he collapses in tears, longing for his son. One of the monks reveals himself to be his son, and the two joyfully reunite. To show his gratitude, the horsetail cutter vows to become a Buddhist monk.

The Tokusa Yama shows the horsetail cutter as the monks encountered him. The float is decorated with *tokusa* horsetail plants, and the metalwork on the float features bats and rabbits. Tokusa plants are harvested in autumn, bats come out at dusk, and Asians see a rabbit in the full moon. These elements lay the scene

THE GION FESTIVAL

of the poem and the season and time that the horsetail cutter met the monks in the noh play.

As we can sense, noh has a strong transcendent element to it; rather than merely acting a scene, noh actors aspire to embody the spirits involved in the play, and transmit the depths of their human and otherworldly experiences and lessons to the audience. This is why Buddhist monks carved statues of noh characters, and why the statues are revered in the Gion Festival.[81] This sacred statue is dated 1692, and signed by a Kasuga Buddhist monk-sculptor from Nara.

Some of Tokusa Yama's rich embroideries show scenes of Taoist Immortals.[82]

On display at Tokusa Yama, this fan painting of a full moon with tokusa plants references the poem, noh play, and Buddhist teaching.

---

[81] See **Ashikari Yama** and **Kikusui Boko** for more about **noh** in the Gion Festival.

[82] For more on Taoism in the Gion Festival, see also **Hakuga Yama**, **Kakkyō Yama**, and **Koi Yama**.

Tōrō Yama 蟷螂山: Brave as a Mantis

On Nishinotōin street, north of Shijō street.

A Chinese proverb relates that a mantis insect is not strong enough to stop an oxcart, but it may be brave enough to try. Tōrō Yama uses a praying mantis and oxcart to honor a courageous 14th-century Kyoto nobleman, Shijō Takasuke. He heroically took on an enemy much stronger than he, the future shōgun Ashikaga Yoshiakira. Shijō was unsuccessful and died in battle. But more than 650 years later his memory lives on through Tōrō Yama.

Everyone delights in the mechanized mantis's movements during the July 17 procession.

The Shijō clan lived in this area, and it's said that Takasuke's family contributed this float to the Gion Festival procession in 1376, 25 years after his death. With a mantis on top of an imperial oxcart, people would have recognized the family's bold tribute. Apparently fearlessness ran in the family.

This float was destroyed several times by fire, including the Great Fire of 1864. Fortunately, the imperial oxcart and mantis survived and were preserved. Since most of Kyoto was destroyed by that fire, it's amazing to imagine how various chōnai managed to save some of their treasures. Dating to 1801, the mantis and oxcart are a kind of mechanized doll called *karakuri ningyō*.

This kind of technology was popular in Japan in the 17th-19th centuries. Imagine what a wonder this mechanization must have been before the industrial revolution. Fast forward more than 100 years after Tōrō Yama last burned, and a master artisan was able to get the mantis and oxcart in working order again. The float was reintroduced to the Gion Festival in 1981, with the popular mantis on its oxcart in full operation during the July 17 procession.

Tamaya Shōbei IX travels from Nagoya each year to manipulate the mantis, which requires four people to operate. The head and legs move, the wings open, and the imperial oxcart's wheels rotate, to the delight of festival visitors. Tōrō Yama is the only float in the Gion Festival to have a *karakuri ningyō*, though floats in other Japanese festivals feature them too. Currently karakuri ningyō are enjoying a revival, as the historic prototype for modern robotics.

Tamaya Shōbei IX—the only living Karakuri Ningyo Master in Japan today from an unbroken lineage—prepares the mantis.

Notice how the oxcart's shafts come out of the mouths of dragon heads, and the golden dragon-fish at the peaks of the Chinese-style roof (see top image). Tōrō Yama may offer the once-in-a-lifetime opportunity to enjoy metalwork decorations in the shape of praying mantises (see **Art Treasures**).

Tōrō Yama's distinctive contemporary yūzen textile decorations.

All four main tapestries are contemporary (1980s-1990s) works by the late yūzen dyeing artist and Living National Treasure, Hata Tokio. Kyoto is famous for its difficult but versatile *yūzen* dyeing technique.

Many yūzen dyers have resided in the Tōrō Yama chōnai, so the textiles honor this connection. It's the only float that has exclusively yūzen decorations.

The Tōrō Yama chōnai has successfully used its float as a rallying point for the neighborhood, making for a lively community with a fresh perspective on the relevance of the Gion Festival for modern people.

Tsuki Boko 月鉾: The Moon Float

On the south side of Shijō street, just west of Muromachi street.

Tsuki Boko is dedicated to Japan's moon god, Tsukiyomi-no-Mikoto. The moon god is the brother and former consort of Japan's sun goddess Amaterasu-Ōmikami. Japan's oldest texts[83] tell us that she became angry and rejected Tsukiyomi because of what she considered his rude behavior. After that, the sun and moon, day and night, were separated forever.

Tsuki means "moon," and this float is easily recognizable by the crescent moon symbol on top of its central *shingi* pole. The deity Tsukiyomi also governs water. Look for aquatic motifs such as waves and seashells in Tsuki Boko's decorations.

This float pays respects to the sun as well, with a three-legged crow above its roof peak and on its members' cotton *yukata,* linen kimono,

---

[83] The early eighth-century *Kojiki* and *Nihon Shōki.*

and *haori* jackets. A two-legged crow is just a bird, a float patron told me, but a three-legged crow is a divine messenger from the sun goddess. The three-legged crow is an ancient mystical symbol related to the sun in Korean and Chinese cultures too.

Unlike many other floats, Tsuki Boko survived the Great Genji Fire of 1864, and so it features many historic treasures. Note the gilt paintings of flowers under the roof eaves, painted in 1784 by artistic genius Maruyama Ōkyo. They all bloom in July, during the Gion Festival. See also gilt paintings of scenes from the world's first novel, *The Tale of Genji*, written in the 11th century by the remarkable court lady Murasaki Shikibu. The scenes are cleverly portrayed within images of fans on the float's ceiling (see image, **Art Treasures**).

While people in the Western hemisphere see an old man in the moon, East Asians see a rabbit. Enjoy the amazing carvings of rabbits leaping amidst golden ocean waves on the roof peaks (see image, **Boarding Yamaboko**). These are attributed to the incredibly versatile, semi-mythical 17th-century artist Hidari Jingorō.[84] The lifelike

---

[84] It's said that Hidari was so skilled that other artisans, overcome with jealousy, cut off his right hand. Fortunately, he was left-handed and continued to design, paint, sculpt, build and teach under the name *Hidari*, which means "left."

metalwork shells are based on designs by Matsumura Keibun (1779-1843) of the Shijō school, named for the studios' street location, the same as Tsuki Boko's. Matsumura also designed decorations for **Niwatori Boko** and **Naginata Boko**.

In the display area, you can see a rare, early 17th-century medallion carpet from Lahore in outstanding condition, a peak representative of Mughal art. It's been likened to an illuminated manuscript of Islam's sacred Koran in woven form. It's believed to be one of a kind: the only other place in the world we can see similar carpets is in 17th-century European oil paintings.

In the same area you'll see beautiful Japanese embroidered textiles of mythical Asian animals: two phoenixes, a griffin, a lion-dog, and of course a blue **dragon**. These were also based on designs by Maruyama Ōkyo, who lived and died near here. Like other hoko, Tsuki Boko used to have a live chigo, but the sacred doll named *Otomaro* took his place in 1912.

Tsuki Boko's unique medallion carpet.

One Tsuki Boko elder described how electric streetcars ran down Shijō Street[85] in the 1950s, when he joined the ohayashi **music** troupe as a young teenager.

---

[85] Japan's first commercial electric streetcars served Kyoto from 1895 until 1978.

The wires were cut each year so the **yamaboko floats** could pass. Sometimes the men pulling the float down below accidentally ran him—a musician sitting high up on the float—into electrical wires that hadn't been cut or otherwise pushed out of the way. "I figured the power had been turned off but I wasn't sure. It was terrifying. I shouted 'Turn the float! Turn the float!' but they can't turn it so easily," he recalled.

Although the streetcars are gone and utility wires have been adapted to the festival, it's still tricky. The men brave enough to stand on the roofs of the **yamaboko floats** during the processions help keep the musicians, floats, and visitors safe.

Urade Yama 占出山: Empress Jingū Divines The Future

On Nishiki-kōji (one block north of Shijō) street, just west of Karasuma street.

Urade Yama shows the third-century Japanese shamaness ruler known as Empress Jingū using fishing as a divining method. She asked the gods to send a fish to let her know if she'd be victorious on a journey to the land of Silla, part of the modern-day Korean peninsula.

This took place on Kyushu Island in western Japan. Closest to the Korean peninsula, Kyushu was home to many settlements of immigrants from the ancient kingdoms that predated Korea.[86]

This float's name, *Urade*, means roughly, "prophesize and go forth." Japan's most ancient texts say Empress Jingū caught a fish, and consequently

*The sacred statue of Empress Jingū wears a **noh** costume and mask, and holds a curved fishing rod.*

---

[86] Immigrants from the modern-day Korean peninsula were highly respected in earliest Japanese history (see **Taishi Yama**). They brought with them technologies like fermentation, ceramic kilns and temple architecture, knowledge like Chinese writing and law, and many other valuable resources.

traveled to Silla. With several gods on her side, the texts tell us, she "conquered" it without fighting. She returned to Japan with abundant tribute.

Besides Urade Yama, **Fune Boko** ("Ship Float") represents Jingū's ship on its way to Silla, and **Ōfune Boko** ("Great Ship Float") is the ship returning, heavy with gifts. One can't help but wonder whether it was this remarkable woman's magnetism that enabled her to win such gains without a battle.

Urade Yama's display area, part of a Shintō shrine.

But Urade Yama's Empress Jingū is prepared for battle, giving us a taste of Japan's little-known but intriguing history of women warriors, *onna-bugeisha*. Both the swords she wears are on display in the treasure area before the July 17 procession. The original *katana* sword is a National Treasure crafted in the tenth century by the legendary Sanjō Munechika, who also created **Naginata Boko**'s mystical longsword.

Urade Yama's **kaisho** treasure display area is unique in that it's located in the lovely, often peaceful courtyard of a sizable Shintō shrine. This shrine and courtyard are only open during the Gion Festival, for Urade Yama. The treasures include textiles depicting Japan's 36 Immortal Poets[87] and its three most famous scenic

---

[87] See **Hoshō Yama** and **Kuronushi Yama** for more on the 36 Immortal Poets.

places, as well as the sweetfish that foretold Jingū's fate. In textiles based on designs by Maruyama-Shijō school artist Suzuki Hyakunen, Korean officials and soldiers puzzle at waters encroaching because of divine tide-controlling jewels Empress Jingū used to land victoriously in Silla.

Look closely to appreciate the quality of Urade Yama's luxurious aristocratic kimono.

Empress Jingū is famous for being pregnant during her bold adventures in Silla, and for giving birth to a healthy baby boy, the next emperor, Ōjin (see **Hachiman Yama**), on her return. Therefore she's considered a protectress of safe childbirth, and amulets are sold here for the same. Over the centuries aristocratic Japanese women used Urade Yama talismans wrapped against their growing bellies to help ensure safe childbirth. After a healthful birth, they gifted their own precious kimono to the deity and her float in gratitude.

Thanks to this tradition, at Urade Yama we can see what kind of kimono Japanese empresses and princesses have worn over the centuries. Passed down through generations, the quality and number of kimono a woman had are still considered a measure of wealth. This makes Empress Jingū and Urade Yama wealthy indeed.

Yamabushi Yama 山伏山: Buddhist Nature Mystics

On Muromachi street, between Nishikikōji and Takoyakushi streets.

Yamabushi translates to "one who prostrates in the mountains." They are practitioners of the 1400-year-old spiritual path called *Shugendō*. Shugendō means "the Way of Training," and involves intense spiritual practices combining Buddhism, Taoism, and Shintō. They hold mountains sacred and do many of their spiritual practices there. People still walk this demanding path today, and contemporary yamabushi come to Yamabushi Yama every year.[88]

Jōzō Kisho blesses Kyoto streets with yamabushi prayers during the July 17 procession.

This float enshrines the brilliant ninth-century yamabushi Jōzō Kisho. He was renowned for the supernatural powers developed through his committed practice. He's most famous for righting the leaning Yasaka pagoda. Considered a terrifying omen at the time, it leaned towards the part of Kyoto where aristocrats lived, foretelling death and

---

[88] For more about yamabushi and Shugendō, see also **En-no-Gyōja Yama**.

THE GION FESTIVAL

destruction for them. Jōzō Kisho spent the night praying at the foot of the pagoda, and by morning it was straight, to everyone's great relief. The fifth-century pagoda still towers upright today, south of Yasaka Shrine (see **Maps**).

Yamabushi Yama is located in a traditional *kyōmachiya* townhouse, and the sacred statue of Jōzō Kisho has pride of place on the second floor. This keeps him above the heads of people on the street, symbolically closer to the heavens. The kyōmachiya houses a business for the rest of the year, but I was told that Jōzō Kisho's room is used for nothing else, quite a commitment in space-challenged Kyoto.

Contemporary yamabushi come at the beginning of every Gion Festival to bless the sacred statue of Jōzō Kisho and the yama's treasures. That way, everyone who walks by benefits from the blessings. Each year on July 15 they also recite the *Heart Sutra* here and hold a fire ritual for world peace, chanting to the beat of a large taiko drum (see

Where else but at the Gion Festival can we join yamabushi in praying for world peace?

Schedule). Walking through the large straw hoop at the kura storehouse in the back purifies our spirits (see **Chimaki**).

This yama has an outstanding collection of antique textiles, some of which were received from the neighboring **Kikusui Boko's chōnai** when the latter float was destroyed in 1864's Great Genji Fire. You can admire them from very close up due to the economy of space. Check out each embroidered stitch, or the lifelike expressions on the woven faces, and imagine how much time it took to acquire the skill to create these highly expressive works. Older kimono for the sacred statue of Jōzō Kisho are also displayed—all noh theater costumes. While there's no direct connection with Yamabushi Yama and **noh theater**,[89] each year the sacred statue is dressed by a professional noh actor, showing the deep historic and cultural connection between the Gion Festival and noh.

Japanese and Chinese embroidered mythical animals, and a "seven treasures" woven net decoration.

During the 2014 Gion Festival, the Yamabushi Yama chōnai innovated its displays to incorporate prayers and fundraising for the Tōhoku region, devastated by the 2011 tsunami. In particular, it supported a permaculture-like shoreline reconstruction project designed to protect against future tsunami. For an 1150-year old festival, how cool is that?

---

[89] There are traditional kyōgen comic theater plays featuring yamabushi. I performed the role of a yamabushi on stage when I studied kyōgen with Living National Treasure Shigeyama Sensaku IV in the early 1990s, in my early years in Kyoto. It was especially challenging because I didn't understand what a yamabushi was.

THE ATO MATSURI: THE "LATER FESTIVAL" JULY 18-24

A highlight of the Ato Matsuri:
Its colorful procession on July 24.

If you're not so keen on crowds or would like a sense of what the Gion Festival was like 50 years ago, the Ato Matsuri is for you.

As mentioned, the Gion Festival floats are divided into two parts. The first is the larger **Saki Matsuri** ("early festival") from July 10-17. Then comes the more intimate *Ato Matsuri* ("later festival") from July 18-24.

The Ato Matsuri is smaller in size (11 floats compared to 23 in the **Saki Matsuri**) and therefore more relaxed. Many festival elders have told me that it reminds them of the Gion Festival from their childhood. How so? The main thing people mention is the feeling that they have the time and space to visit and spend time with one another. Despite appearances, this is a community-based festival. And isn't connection something that every living thing seeks?

*A yamabushi from **En-no-Gyōja Yama** watches floats passing during the July 24 procession.*

From a Shintō perspective, the Kyoto townspeople use the Saki Matsuri floats as a way to welcome the **Yasaka Shrine deities** to purify downtown Kyoto during their journey to and stay at the *otabisho*, July 17-24. The Ato Matsuri floats' procession on July 24 expresses thanks to the deities for their visit and blessings, and a ritual farewell.

In both the Saki and Ato Matsuri processions, each of the float's own deities also ritually cleanses the energy of downtown, townspeople, and visitors. This is partly to prepare for the deities' travel from or to Yasaka Shrine, and partly for the benefit of all. These two objectives are fundamentally one and the same.

It all sounds so spiritual. But relatively few people today are aware of this spiritual foundation of the Gion Festival sensory extravaganza. It's also likely that, throughout history, many people have participated in the Gion Festival more for social connections, history, and culture, or just for the fun of it.

But human beings seek meaning, and the Gion Festival is a wellspring of it. The struggle of seeking meaning but not finding it is the beginning of every Hero's Journey, every wisdom tradition worldwide. The realization that meaning is all around us is the fruit of every such path. Visiting the Gion Festival with this knowledge touches us with a profound beauty that stays with us all our lives.

*The **Yasaka Shrine deities** emanate blessings from their **mikoshi** at the otabisho "visiting place" July 17-24, at the Shijō-Teramachi intersection (see **Maps**).*

WHAT'S THE ATO MATSURI TIMELINE?

The Ato Matsuri's yamaboko floats are constructed and the treasure display areas get organized beginning from July 18th with **Ōfune Boko**. Then from July 19th communities begin building the large hiki-yama, **Minami**

Yamaboko Tate *float construction will forever change your perspective on rope and knots.* **Kita Kannon Yama**.

Kannon Yama and **Kita Kannon Yama**, plus **Koi Yama**. The remaining seven yama begin construction and treasure display on July 20th.

On July 20 from about 14:30, the three **yamaboko floats** on Shinmachi street[90] simultaneously have **hikizome,** a test pull to make sure all is working well. Anyone can participate, so this is your chance to see what pulling a float is like. It's good fun and maybe not what you'd expect. Pay attention and take care of your physical safety. Of all the smaller yama in the festival, only **Hashi Benkei Yama** has a *kakizome* practice "shouldering" by its chōnai members, at 9:00 on July 21. The float gets decorated in preparation and dismantled again afterward.

Everyone loves **hikizome**, *here in the lovely ambiance of the* **Minami Kannon Yama** *chōnai.*

Watching chōnai members assemble and disassemble their floats can be fascinating. **Hashi Benkei Yama.**

All the floats and their treasures are on display to the public on July 21, 22, and 23, from about 9:00 until

---

[90] **Ōfune Boko, Minami Kannon Yama,** and **Kita Kannon Yama**.

around 21:00. The excitement builds with the Ato Matsuri's **yoiyoiyoiyama, yoiyoiyama,** and **yoiyama** on the evenings of July 21-23.

The ohayashi **music** troupes from the three yamaboko on Shinmachi street—**Ōfune Boko**, **Minami Kannon Yama**, and **Kita Kannon Yama**—plus **Taka Yama** on Sanjō street play music until 22:00 or 23:00 on those nights.

The **Kita Kannon Yama** ohayashi *music* troupe plays during *yoiyama*.

On July 23 from about 21:30, those four ohayashi **music** troupes walk along Shijō street with paper lanterns to the *otabisho* "visiting place" at the Shijō-Teramachi intersection, to pray to the **Yasaka Shrine deities** for good weather during the July 24 procession. It's a ritual called *Hiyori Kagura*, meaning literally, "Good Weather Music for the Deities," and they play music all the way. Then at 23:00, the **Minami Kannon Yama** chōnai performs its wild Abare-Kannon ritual.

*A private home in the **Hachiman Yama chōnai** generously displays a family heirloom, painted by Yokoyama Kazan, in the **Byōbu Matsuri**.*

Meanwhile, local residents and companies share the spirit by displaying their own private treasures, in a July 21-23 sub festival called the ***Byōbu Matsuri*** or "folding screen festival." Partly because the Ato Matsuri is smaller than the **Saki Matsuri**, Ato Matsuri *chōnai* put extra effort into creating an attractive, traditional festival ambiance. Recently increasing numbers of homes and businesses decorate their street front with paper lanterns and umbrellas. The *yatai* food and game street stalls are not allowed in the Ato Matsuri, making for a very different atmosphere compared to the **Saki Matsuri**.

*Yoiyama in the **Kita Kannon Yama** chōnai.*

The Ato Matsuri Floats Procession and Hanagasa Junkō

The Ato Matsuri begins on Oike street, against a backdrop of cool greenery.

The Ato Matsuri peaks on July 24 with the *yamaboko junkō* or floats' procession. Starting at 9:30 on Oike street, the floats seem to sail amidst the waters of the trees' cool green leaves. The visuals are dazzling, and the smaller number of floats allows us to enjoy the whole procession despite the heat. Try to catch the larger floats doing **Tsuji Mawashi**—it's a high achievement in cooperation and perhaps the most amazing corner-turning

THE GION FESTIVAL

experience on the planet. Note that the Ato Matsuri floats' procession route is the same as the **Saki Matsuri procession**, but in the opposite direction (see **Maps**).

Minami Kannon Yama prepares for **Tsuji Mawashi**.

Kyoto's *hana-machi "flower town"* geisha communities and other traditional arts professionals are central to the lovely **Hanagasa Junkō** (Flower Umbrella Procession). It takes place at the same time as the Ato Matsuri procession, beginning at 10:00. At some points, the two processions' routes overlap (see **Maps**). In the afternoon the geiko-san and other performers grace the **Yasaka Shrine** stage with their elegant **performing arts**.

On the night of July 24, we can enjoy the raucous *kankō-sai* ritual downtown. While the kankōsai and **shinkōsai** have lower profiles than

Gion geiko-san and other performing artists enrich the **Hanagasa Junkō**.

the yamaboko floats, they are central to the spiritual meaning of the festival.

During the kankōsai, hundreds of men return the main three Gion Festival deities in their portable *mikoshi* shrines from central Kyoto back to Yasaka

Shrine. After their return, around 23:00, the entire shrine is darkened for the *mitama utsushi* ("spirit transfer") ritual. The **deities** are mysteriously conveyed from

*Kyoto residents take to the streets to celebrate the **Yasaka Shrine deities** passing by in their portable **mikoshi** shrines, and to cheer on the men who carry them.*

the mikoshi back to their usual home inside the *honden* main hall.

See the **Schedule** for details.

On July 25 kyōgen —a traditional form of comic theater—is performed at Yasaka Shrine. Then on July 28, the *mikoshi* are ritually cleansed with blessed waters from the Kamo River in a closing **mikoshi arai** ceremony.

Lastly, the Gion Festival officially ends on July 31, with a final cleansing ritual at the small "Epidemic Shrine" within **Yasaka Shrine**. It's a manifestation of the Somin Shōrai legend that also gave birth to the omnipresent Gion Festival **chimaki** talisman. Anyone may jump through the straw hoop that cleanses our spirits one more time, signifying rebirth for another year.

En-no-Gyōja Yama 役行者山: Shugendō's Founder

On Muromachi street, south of Aneyakōji street.

This yama pays respects to En-no-Gyōja or "En the Ascetic," the semi-legendary seventh-century founder of *Shugendō*. Today practitioners known as *yamabushi* still follow this spiritual belief system of rigorous practices, which include hiking routes in the shape of sacred mandalas in nature. They consider En-no-Gyōja a *bodhisattva*, someone who delays nirvana to devote all their energy to benefit all beings. Shugendō's

The sacred statue of En-no-Gyōja (center), with the goddess Katsuragi on the right and the god Hitokotonushi at left.

esoteric philosophy, esteem for the power of nature, and intense training have inspired the likes of beat poet Gary Snyder. Though these followers' commitment is deep, they remain lay people, making it an accessible path.

The sacred statue of En-no-Gyōja holds a shakujō—a pilgrim's staff that doubles as a martial arts weapon (see image above). During the July 24 procession, his other hand holds a scroll of a Buddhist sutra.

Modern-day yamabushi visit En-no-Gyōja Yama every year to pay respects to their extraordinary founder, and to pray for world peace. Join in for a truly unique experience (see **Schedule**).[91]

As a young man, this original mountain ascetic trained and gained profound realization on Mt. Katsuragi, in the Yoshino district of neighboring Nara Prefecture.[92] Legends say that the power generated by En-no-Gyōja's ascetic practices gave him supernatural gifts, including healing and commanding gods, demons, and humans.

Contemporary yamabushi chant the Heart Sutra for world peace and perform a goma-taki fire ritual at En-no-Gyōja Yama every year on July 23 around 14:15. You too may write a prayer on one of the small wooden sticks that later get ritually blessed and burned. Available at En-no-Gyōja Yama.

This yama also enshrines the sacred statues of two deities (see above image), who En-no-Gyōja directed to construct a bridge between the sacred peaks of Mt. Katsuragi and nearby Mt. Kinpusen. As the legend goes, these two felt so ashamed of their unattractive appearance that they only worked on the bridge between the two peaks at night. The deity who looks like a demon is named *Hitokotonushi*, which intriguingly translates in English to, "The One Primary Word." The goddess's

---

[91] See the **Yamabushi Yama** pages for more about yamabushi.
[92] It's said that En-no-Gyōja survived during this time in the wilderness on pine needles and wild fruit. Yamabushi still practice there today, in the mystical region called Yoshino.

THE GION FESTIVAL

name is *Katsuragi*, after one of the sacred mountain peaks: she is likely the resident deity. This name means "Arrowroot[93] Fortress" in English.

The sacred statue of Katsuragi holds a Buddhist *chakraratna* or "wheel jewel," an eight-spoked wheel-shaped treasure symbolizing the Buddha's Ennobling Eightfold Path. Possession of this treasure is said to make journeys effortless. Hitokotonushi holds a golden ax.

Step through the purifying straw hoop around the entrance into En-no-Gyōja Yama's spacious courtyard **kaisho** display area, with two *kura* storehouses: the deities are enshrined in one.

This yama has an unusually diverse collection of historic treasures on display. Besides amazing metalwork (enjoy the end caps of the round poles), you'll see numerous antique Chinese tapestries depicting dragons, and painted scrolls of the yama over the centuries. Note the scroll/map of locations of Gion Festival **yamaboko floats** throughout history. It shows names and locations of yamaboko that no longer exist, a valuable resource to help us understand the Gion Festival's past.

---

[93] The arrowroot plant—*kudzu* in Japanese—has healing properties still used in contemporary Japan.

Hachiman Yama 八幡山: Protector of Warriors

On Shinmachi street, between Rokkaku and Sanjō streets.

Hachiman Yama is dedicated to Hachiman, the Shintō god of war and protector of Japan and the Japanese people. The semi-legendary, third-century Emperor Ōjin was so greatly revered that he was deified as Hachiman.

Japan's most ancient texts tell Ōjin's life story, beginning with his birth to Empress Jingū.[94] Known for centralizing power, Ōjin also developed cultural exchanges with modern-day Korea and China. All this led to a flourishing of Japanese culture.

In the 11th century, Hachiman was adopted as the guardian deity of the Minamoto clan, of *The Tale of the Heike* fame.[95] He soon became the patron deity of all samurai. Interestingly the food-producing class also worshipped him as the deity of agriculture and fisheries. This broad and deep appeal made Hachiman one of the most revered gods in Japan, with more than 30,000 shrines.

---

[94] His mother Empress Jingū is revered at **Ōfune Boko, Fune Boko,** and **Urade Yama.**

[95] See **Hashi Benkei Yama** and **Jōmyō Yama** for more on the Minamoto clan and *The Tale of the Heike.*

THE GION FESTIVAL

Note the float's stunningly well-crafted gold-leaf shrine to Hachiman, with a permanent Shintō shrine opposite. The original float shrine is attributed to the 12th-13th-century genius monk-sculptor Unkei, though this one dates to the late 1700s.

Hachiman's messenger is the dove, and you'll see this bird among the float's treasures. Two small dove sculptures that rest on the Shintō *torii* gate during the July 24 procession are attributed to the legendary 17th-century artist Hidari Jingorō.[96] Curiously the god of war's dove is said to help couples maintain harmonious relations, and talismans are sold here for the same.

Hachiman Yama's eye-catching treasure display area. Note the gold shrine at left.

Hachiman Yama's treasures also feature a recently digitized replica of its rare 17th-century folding byōbu screen depicting the Gion Festival's **Ato Matsuri**. A rare survivor of Kyoto's 1788 Great Tenmei Fire, such artworks offer valuable insights into the Gion Festival's distant past.

Hachiman Yama's **chōnai** is blessed with diverse treasures, and a strong enough community spirit to showcase them well. In addition to its collection of antique and contemporary textiles, metalwork, painting, documents, and sculptures, chōnai members cooperate to enhance the local atmosphere during the

---

[96] See **Tsuki Boko** for more on the artist Hidari.

Gion Festival. Several homes display historic folding byōbu screens, making this one of the best chōnai for the **Byōbu Matsuri**.

*Look closely at Hachiman Yama's folding screen to make out different floats still in the festival today, plus the **kankōsai** procession of portable **mikoshi** shrines.*

Remember that our Gion Festival hosts are busy modern people just like us. They're generous too: They take the time and energy to keep these artworks in good condition (a costly undertaking), and bear the risk to share them with us. Though we may see the fruits of their efforts for only a week or two, it's a year-round, long-term, multigenerational commitment.

In 2015 the Hachiman Yama chōnai collaborated with Ritsumeikan University's Art Research Center to digitally measure the float's component parts and construction. It's a forward-looking development in this ancient festival. As the social fabric of intergenerational communities thins in downtown Kyoto, traditions are conveyed less and less by direct hands-on experience and word of mouth. Procuring digital imagery and measurements helps support year-round research and planning to ensure we can celebrate the Gion Festival for centuries to come.

HASHI BENKEI YAMA 橋弁慶山: LOYALTY AND THE TALE OF THE HEIKE

On Takoyakushi street, west of Karasuma street.

The first float in the Ato Matsuri by ancient tradition, Hashi Benkei Yama depicts a famous scene in Japanese history. In 1174, the giant warrior-monk[97] Benkei had a personal quest to collect 1000 swords by defeating 1000 samurai. As his final match, he challenged a small boy named Ushiwakamaru. Hashi Benkei Yama portrays their history-changing battle on the nearby Gojō Bridge.

Ushiwakamaru was born into the Minamoto clan of the famed *Tale of the Heike*.[98] Fearing he'd be killed by the enemy Taira clan, his mother abandoned him on mystical Mt. Kurama in northern Kyoto. On Mt. Kurama, a

The kakizome *test run on July 21. Hashi Benkei is the only kaki- (shoulder-borne) yama to do this, and the only* **chōnai** *members who move their assembled float themselves.*

---

[97] The tradition of *sōhei* warrior monks is strongly linked to the esoteric Tendai Buddhist school's Enryaku-ji Temple on the sacred Mt. Hiei in northeastern Kyoto. Sōhei have similarities with European crusading orders. Benkei was also a yamabushi (see **En-no-Gyōja Yama**) for a time, not unusual for sōhei.

[98] This epic tale has been called "a Japanese *Iliad*."

supernatural being known as Tengu raised Ushiwakamaru, training him in magical martial arts. Benkei was at least twice Ushiwakamaru's size, famously strong, and an experienced, gifted warrior. However, the boy won easily and even gracefully, balancing on the bridge's rail posts while fighting.

The sacred statue of Ushiwakamaru balances on a bridge post while battling Benkei, as the real Ushiwakamaru reportedly did in the 12th century.

Ultimately Benkei was so impressed by the boy's incredible abilities that he laid down his weapons, bowed to the ground, and swore eternal loyalty. Later Ushiwakamaru became known as the great Minamoto clan general Yoshitsune. Benkei faithfully served him until they died together, betrayed in battle 17 years later. They rank among the most beloved figures in Japanese history.

The two sacred statues are signed and dated "1563" by Kō-un of the Kei school of sculpture, renowned for extraordinary sculptors who were also committed Buddhist monks. The Ushiwakamaru statue balances on the front tooth of one tall, two-toothed *geta* sandal, an incredible sculptural feat for the time.

This float's treasures are still displayed annually in a traditional **kyōmachiya** townhouse. In this type of Gion Festival-specific architecture, sacred statues are displayed on the second floor. This builds this sign of respect—raising that which is sacred above our heads—into construction. Traditionally it's also believed that positive energy radiates from the sacred statues of these Japanese heroes during the  festival. With the deities higher up, it's easier for any beneficial energy to shower upon people going by.

Note the beautiful metalwork of birds flying among dynamic waves on the black lacquered bridge. Qing imperial court costumes with embroidered dragons from the early and mid-1700s were long ago upcycled into stunning float decorations. The 1809 textiles of Kyoto's Aoi Matsuri processions on the float's sides (see top image) are believed to be based on designs by Maruyama Ōkyo.[99]

Hashi Benkei Yama's **chōnai** members bravely went through centuries of their historic records and input them into a computer for future generations. In the process, they found documents their chōnai members wrote after Kyoto's 1864 Great Genji Fire. These included letters to other Gion Festival chōnai, inquiring whether they and their floats had survived and were able to take part in the next Gion Festival. Hashi Benkei Yama was one of few floats able to participate in the following year's procession.

---

[99] See **Niwatori Boko** for more on Maruyama Ōkyo.

Jōmyō Yama 浄妙山: Incredible Warrior Monks

On Rokkaku street, between Karasuma and Muromachi streets.

Jōmyō Yama shows two renowned *sōhei*[100] warrior monks, Tsutsui Jōmyō and Ichirai Hōshi, at The Battle at the Bridge, a famous scene from the Battle of Uji. This conflict started the 12th-century Genpei War between the Minamoto and Heike clans, as told in *The Tale of the Heike* epic.

It was May 1180 on Uji Bridge,[101] a strategic crossing on the way to Kyoto. These warrior monks were defending the Minamoto clan from a crowd of oncoming Heike samurai. The Minamoto troops had pulled planks off one side of the bridge so that the enemy Heike couldn't cross. The Heike managed to get over the Uji River on foot and horseback instead.

Ichirai leaps over his fellow warrior monk, Jōmyō, to get to battle. Note the strip of river waters carved in wood below them, and the textile showing Uji Bridge.

---

[100] See **Hashi Benkei Yama** for more on *sōhei*.
[101] Among other things, Uji is famous for growing green tea for the ancient capital: any green tea you drink in Kyoto is probably from Uji. It's also home to the extraordinary Byōdō-in Temple, depicted on the back of the 10-yen coin.

The fighting was intense, represented by all the arrows on the float.

The bridge was narrow, warriors were many, and the junior monk Ichirai got trapped at the far end, away from the action. Moving with courage, determination, and acrobatic prowess, he catapulted over the head of the senior monk Jōmyō in front of him, to get to the front lines. Ichirai could thus also protect his elder, Jōmyō, and generate merit[102] thereby.

It's said that Ichirai excused himself for his bad manners as he leaped over Jōmyō's head. Consequently, for a time Jōmyō Yama's nickname was the "Pardon Me Float."

During the July 24th procession, notice how the sacred statues of Ichirai and Jōmyō tremble as Jōmyō Yama moves. All the weight of Ichirai's sacred statue, plus its armor, is borne by the arm. The sculptor defied gravity by giving it a body-shaped wood "skeleton." The two sacred statues are held together with a wooden wedge: in the treasure display area, you can see it on Ichirai's left hand.

The Tale of the Heike records how Jōmyō and Ichirai fought with bow and arrow, halberd,[103] sword, and dagger. Jōmyō wielded each in turn until they broke, the story goes, felling 38 enemy men. He continued

---

[102] Generating merit is a central belief in Buddhism. It's similar to sowing seeds of good karma.

[103] The halberd or *naginata* is a sōhei warrior monks' signature weapon. Curiously, besides sōhei, only women used naginata. One is also attached to the top of the **Naginata Boko** central *shingi* pole.

fighting even after he was shot through with over 60 arrows, all sticking out from his samurai armor.

Note Jōmyō Yama's beautiful new **textiles** depicting the Uji Bridge, based on famous Momoyama (1568-1600) paintings by Hasegawa Tōhaku. The similar piece with a *sakura* cherry blossom tree is based on a painting by the master painter Hasegawa and his son, Kyūzō, designated a National Treasure. Gion Festival chōnai can receive funding from the national government to make replicas of antique **textiles**, but not for creating new ones. New textiles are an important way to support Kyoto's living textile tradition and maintain creative diversity in the Gion Festival. See also the striking

***Kyōmachiya** in the Jōmyō Yama chōnai.*

folding screens in the treasure area, depicting Jōmyō and Ichirai in battle. They were painted by Suzuki Shōnen, a leading artist from the turn of the last century.

Enjoy Jōmyō Yama's pleasant chōnai atmosphere. They've conserved numerous traditional **kyōmachiya** buildings and a family-oriented neighborhood feeling.

KITA KANNON YAMA 北観音山: NORTHERN KANNON FLOAT

On Shinmachi street, south of Rokkaku street.

Kita Kannon Yama is one of the most traditional floats and **chōnai** in the Gion Festival. Only chōnai members and their guests may visit the float, pay respects to its deity, and view its treasures. Nothing is on sale, and only men may board the float. I used to live next door and this was the first float I ever saw,[104] so you could say it's the reason you're reading this book.

One elder told me that they don't open their treasure display area or sell festival-related goods to the public because they'd like their chōnai to be able to enjoy the festival as they always have. Conservation is expensive, and the area's rich kimono merchants are

Take time to enjoy the wonder of the music and the beauty and craftsmanship of each decorative element.

---

[104] The small covered doorway between the white *kura* storehouse and Kita Kannon Yama's treasure display area is the entrance to a long walkway that went to my former home and garden, before they were demolished to build an apartment building. Part of the garden—a lovely small persimmon grove—was preserved for apartment residents.

mostly a thing of the past, so this is an impressive accomplishment. Some of Kita Kannon Yama's chōnai members have directed energy towards retaining the original atmosphere as a neighborhood event. As a result, this chōnai features several traditional buildings, including some of the most beautiful and generous **Byōbu Matsuri** displays in the festival. We could say that they've chosen to share their float and treasures with the public in different ways.

Yōryū Kannon, specializing in compassion, healing, and disaster prevention.

As the name suggests, this float is dedicated to Kannon, the Buddhist bodhisattva of compassion.[105] Kannon appears in 33 different forms, and here she is *Yōryū* or "Willow Tree" Kannon. Traditionally people prayed to her for recovery from illness,[106] and made offerings of willow twigs to prevent disasters. With the summer storms and related illnesses that motivated the original Gion Festival, we can see why Yōryū Kannon was popular. Antibiotics came to Kyoto in the late 1940s, meaning

---

[105] A bodhisattva is a person who delays Buddhahood in order to work for the benefit of all beings. See **Minami Kannon Yama** for more about Kannon, known as Kwan Yin in China and Avalokiteshvara in India.

[106] Willow has been used for thousands of years to treat pain, fever, and inflammation, some of the symptoms of illnesses that Kyotoites suffered during the summer rainy season.

that today's festival elders remember summer illnesses and deaths from their youth.[107] Since we know the float was first constructed in 1353, this chōnai has had a relationship with Kannon for close to 700 years.

This chōnai is named "Rokkaku-chō," after the nearby Rokkaku street and temple. *Rokkaku* means "six corners," and the beautiful Rokkaku-dō Temple[108] has six sides. Consequently you'll see hexagon shapes on chōnai members' clothing and fans.

Kita Kannon Yama, **Minami Kannon Yama**, and **Iwatō Yama** form a small group of *hiki-yama* or "pulled yama" that look like hoko. Once reconstructed, nearby **Taka Yama** will join them. What marks these floats as yama is the pine coming out of their center: hoko have a central bamboo *shingi* (literally, "gods' tree") topped by a metal symbol.[109]

Kita Kannon Yama's *mi-okuri*—the long textile on the rear of the floats during their processions—is a late 17th-century Chinese weaving that looks freshly made. Purchased in 1986, it's said that it was stored in a Tibetan monastery for centuries, and never saw the light of day. Its plant-based colors are extremely vibrant—very rare for such an old piece. Even its brief exposure to Kyoto's summer sun and humidity

---

[107] Ironically, the year this book was written, the floats' processions and other major aspects of the Gion Festival were canceled due to the coronavirus pandemic.

[108] The temple was founded by Shōtoku Taishi in the sixth century (see **Taishi Yama**) and has ancient connections with ikebana flower arrangement (see **Niwatori Boko**).

[109] For a refresher on the difference between yama and hoko, see the **Yama and Hoko Floats Explained** section.

pains professional art conservationists. But it allows the rest of us to better imagine what other antique textiles in the festival looked like when they were new, hundreds of years ago.[110]

Willow branches hang from the back of the float during the July 24 procession. They're given as popular talismans to festival-goers right afterward. Note the colorful mi-okuri *textile, plus the central pine tree pole.*

---

[110] To compare, check out **Kuronushi Yama's** similar piece in very fine condition, but with exposure to the elements. It also has a new replica.

Koi Yama 鯉山: The Carp That Became a Dragon

On Muromachi street, between Takoyakushi and Rokkaku streets.

Koi Yama features a Shintō shrine together with a large wooden carving of a carp (*koi* in Japanese). The shrine is dedicated to Susano-o-no-Mikoto, the **main deity of Yasaka Shrine** and the Gion Festival. The carp swims through a Shintō *torii* gate and up carved wooden waves combined with spun hemp, representing a waterfall.

The fish refers to an ancient Sino-Japanese legend about a carp that persevered in swimming up a waterfall. When it finally, miraculously reached the top, it transformed into a celestial dragon and flew off into the sky.

Koi Yama's metalwork depicts waves for the koi to swim.

Koi Yama uses "Climb the Dragon's Gate" as shorthand for this story, which may have originated at the Dragon's Gate waterfall in Guizhou, China. This site was also where the Dragon Gate School of Taoism began in the 12th century.[111]

---

[111] We know from textiles depicting Taoist Immortals—see **Hakuga Yama**, **Kakkyō Yama**, and **Tokusa Yama** for example—that the Gion Festival community was interested in Taoism centuries ago. Whether the interest was cultural,

The legend has made koi a popular folklore symbol in Japan, inspiring us to overcome any daunting odds. "Climbing the dragon's gate" can mean rising to success from a lowly station, as well as achieving Buddhahood. The latter would make the carp a symbol of kundalini energy rising up the spine at the moment of enlightenment.

*Oral tradition holds that the sacred carp statue was carved by the incredible 17th-century artist Hidari Jingorō (see **Tsuki Boko**).*

Koi Yama's Belgian tapestry was long ago divided up and rearranged to fit the different sizes of the various sides of its float. The aesthetic differs from Western tastes, with an aim to delight and dazzle the eye. In 1979 the Koi Yama **chōnai** commissioned research on this tapestry from Belgium's Royal Museum of Fine Arts. It found that the Gion Festival boasts three 16th-century tapestries from a larger set,[112] all showing a "B.B."

---

intellectual, or spiritual remains unclear. The Dragon Gate School combines Taoism with Buddhism and Confucianism. The Gion Festival would have added Shintō to the mix.

[112] One other is shared between **Niwatori Boko** and **Arare Tenjin Yama**, with a portion of a third at **Hakurakuten Yama**. Other tapestries or fragments from this set decorate floats in the Otsu Festival and the Nagahama Hikiyama Festival, while another is conserved in the Maeda Ikutokukai Foundation in Tokyo.

mark standing for "Brussels City, Braban State." These are the only known examples worldwide of this kind of tapestry depicting scenes from the Trojan War and Homer's *The Iliad*.[113] Koi Yama's main panel shows King Priam and Queen Hecuba of Troy.

These tapestries were likely gifts from Pope Paolo V to Sendai daimyō Date Masamune's little-known but fascinating diplomatic/trade mission to Europe in the early 1600s. Hasekura Tsunenaga led Date's representatives to visit the Philippines, New Spain (now Mexico), and Europe. They met personages like the King of Spain and the Pope. The tapestries were most likely gifts from the same to the man they believed was the King of Japan. The textiles entered Japan and were seized as contraband just as the Tokugawa shōgun closed Japan to limit foreign influence. How they went from there to the Gion Festival remains to be discovered.

*Historic and new chōnai members share their treasures with the public in their traditional **kyōmachiya**.*

Koi Yama's chōnai has created an excellent pamphlet and booklet on Koi Yama, with some good English. Among other things, the booklet shares how

---

[113] See **Kankō Boko** for another Belgian tapestry of similar style and era in excellent condition, but with an Old Testament Biblical theme, and a different journey to the Gion Festival.

chōnai residents had dwindled to just 21 in 1995. With the addition of a large apartment building, chōnai residents rocketed to 280 people within ten years. Koi Yama's chōnai had the foresight to plan how to help new residents integrate well with its Gion Festival traditions (see **Stepping Into the Challenge**).

Kuronushi Yama 黒主山: An Immortal Poet

On Muromachi street, between Rokkaku and Sanjō streets.

The tenth-century Ōtomo-no-Kuronushi was one of the Six Immortal Poets of the early Heian period. His poetry was considered so wonderful that he was posthumously deified.[114]

In a *yōkyoku* song called "Shiga," chanted in **noh theater**, an old man paused one afternoon to enjoy the beauty of *sakura* cherry blossoms, and recited one of Kuronushi's poems. Because the beauty of sakura blossoms is sublime but short-lived, they're a symbol for the impermanence of this world. The song tells us that, as night fell, the god of poetry appeared, celebrating the fleeting beauty of life with sacred dance.

Kuronushi Yama celebrates Japan's passion for poetry and sakura cherry blossoms. The central Chinese dragon textile dates to the 16th century.

Sometime after Kuronushi's death, a politically motivated campaign successfully damaged his

---

[114] A shrine is dedicated to the poet in the neighboring province of Shiga, where he was a local lord.

reputation. Today, few of his poems are readily available. However, this surviving poem surely refers to sakura:

The spring rain
Could that be people's tears,
Since there is no one
Who does not grieve
Over the falling blossoms?

The poet's name, *Kuronushi*, means "The Black Lord." Many of Kuronushi Yama's float decorations are covered in shiny black lacquer, unique in the festival.

A respected Kuronushi Yama elder told me that, before the 15th-century Ōnin War, the yama was called "Saigyō Yama." Saigyō Hōshi was a 12th-century samurai who left worldly life to become a monk. He left many poems describing time alone in nature, including the splendor of sakura. These flowers are also a common metaphor for the glory of youthful samurai warriors, whose lives often came to a sudden end.

Sakura-viewing bliss. Note the sacred statue's beautiful kimono, a noh costume.

Perhaps Kuronushi Yama illustrates one of Saigyō's most famous poems:

I wish to die in spring
under cherry-blossoms
in the time of the spring full moon.

Saigyō is also the subject of three noh plays.[115] In one, *Saigyō's Cherry Tree,* the monk-poet recites a poem complaining about unrefined crowds who come to admire his magnificent ancient tree's blossoms. The spirit of the tree appears to Saigyō as an old man and suggests he purify his perspective: "The eyes can see any spot of the world as sorrows or as a mountain retreat: that depends wholly on the seer's own heart."[116]

Unique in the festival, a host at Kuronushi Yama helpfully explains its treasures to the public (in Japanese only).

Like many yamaboko, Saigyō Yama was destroyed in the decade-long Ōnin War. When the float was relaunched, the chōnai elder explained, it had the name Kuronushi Yama. Why or how that change occurred is still unclear. While the elderly man shown enjoying cherry blossoms on Kuronushi Yama is generally

---

[115] Two were authored by the genius playwright Zeami. See **Ashikari Yama** for more on Zeami.
[116] Royall Tyler, *Japanese No Dramas,* (London: Penguin Books, 1992) p 220.

believed to be the Black Lord, he could be Saigyō, or perhaps the spirit of Saigyō's ancient sakura tree.

Enjoy the remarkable collection of Chinese textiles in Kuronushi Yama's spacious display area. Some original textiles and their reproductions are together, so we can compare colors, condition, and quality.

The imitation sakura branches on this float are given away after the July 24 procession as talismans: It's said that sakura at your door will keep harm away.

Minami Kannon Yama 南観音山: The Southern Kannon Float

On Shinmachi street, between Nishikikōji and Takoyakushi streets.

Minami Kannon Yama joins **Kita Kannon Yama** in celebrating Kannon, the Buddhist bodhisattva of compassion.[117] Their names mean the Southern and Northern Kannon Floats, respectively, referring to their positions along Shinmachi street.

Both revere *Yōryū* or "Willow" Kannon, who alleviates suffering and specializes in healing. Willow branches hang from the back of the float during the July 24 procession, helping spread healing throughout downtown Kyoto. Round wooden tassel holders at the floats' corners feature carved designs of medicinal plants. This float and **Ōfune Boko** are the only ones the public can board during the **Ato Matsuri**.

Minami Kannon Yama presents a lovely evening ambiance.

Minami Kannon Yama boasts a stunningly beautiful sacred statue of Kannon, accompanied by Zenzai Dōji, a manifestation of Manjusri, the bodhisattva

---

[117] Devotion to Kannon has been greatly popular over space and time. She's known as Kwan Yin in China, and in male form as Avalokiteshvara in India, and Chenrezig in Tibet.

of wisdom.[118] Taking photos of sacred statues is discouraged, but it's worth visiting the treasure display area—in a tastefully recreated modern **kyōmachiya**—to see them.

Other treasures on display may include four 19th-century embroidered panels of a dragon, tiger, phoenix, and tortoise, based on designs by artist Shiokawa Bunrin. These animals relate to each of the four directions in Japanese feng shui. You'll recognize the blue **dragon** of the east and Yasaka Shrine. It's also depicted on the large tapestry decorating the back of this float based on designs by 20th-century artist Kayama Matazō.

Minami Kannon Yama's chōnai strikes a fine balance between tradition and innovation. They hold Gion Festival study groups for **chōnai** youth so that everyone in the neighborhood understands its festival culture. They're trying some interesting culture-based approaches to fundraising to support their float.[119] Minami Kannon Yama also includes female musicians in its **ohayashi music** troupe.

---

[118] See **Kita Kannon Yama** for more on Kannon and bodhisattvas.

[119] As mentioned, changes in Kyoto's downtown core and the kimono industry mean that the longstanding tradition of wealthy merchants supporting the floats is a thing of the past. However, there's not yet a new financial model to replace it.

Kyōmachiya and Architectural Conservation

Kudos go to the Minami Kannon Yama **chōnai** community for its active conservation and re-creation of traditional ***kyōmachiya*** townhouses. Since the early 1990s, the neighborhood association has successfully pioneered conservation and restoration of downtown Kyoto's traditional cityscape ambiance. To this end, they've also blocked apartment buildings from being constructed. See **Stepping into the Challenge** in the **Community** section for more.

Minami Kannon Yama's chōnai combines original buildings with new construction featuring culturally-sensitive designs to retain the feel of Kyoto's historical cityscape.

This chōnai's architecture and design finesse have extended towards displaying their art treasures to the public. Note the unusual display cases along the street, where the public can view antique textiles. In one, people in winged costumes and masks perform ceremonial court *bugaku* dance. A rare 17th-century Persian Safavid carpet on display is a style called "Polonaise."

Minami Kannon Yama's rituals include what may be the Gion Festival floats' wildest. On July 23 at 23:00—after more than a week of Gion Festival festivities and with the Ato Matsuri procession starting early the next morning—the **Minami Kannon Yama** chōnai members place their sacred statue of Kannon on a platform, hoist it onto their shoulders, and run up and down through the crowds on their street block several times. The sacred statue of Kannon is all wrapped up, presumably to protect her, so we only see her silhouette.

Called *Abare Kannon,* the ritual involves men shaking and turning the platform Kannon is on, to scatter the blessings near and far.[120] We too can receive Kannon's blessings, while watching in amazement. Does this unusual night ritual call on Kannon's compassion to protect us from the darkness? Or does it invite compassion into our dream world?

---

[120] During the **shinkōsai** and **kankōsai**—arguably the other wildest parts of the Gion Festival—the men celebrate the Yasaka Shrine deities in their **mikoshi** by shaking them in the same way.

ŌFUNE BOKO 大船鉾: THE GREAT SHIP FLOAT

On Shinmachi street, south of Shijō street.

Ōfune Boko is the only hoko in the **Ato Matsuri**, and one of the shining stars of the Gion Festival. Why? In 2014, the long-absent **Ōfune Boko** and the Ato Matsuri were reintroduced together, a joyful time for Gion Festival fans. It and **Minami Kannon Yama** are the only floats the public can board during the Ato Matsuri.

*The new Ōfune Boko prepares for **tsuji mawashi** corner-turning on its inaugural journey in July 2014.*

Ōfune Boko was destroyed in 1864's Great Genji Fire, and only some of its treasures survived. Conversations about reconstruction began in the late 1990s. Economic and social conditions of those times were tough: the economic bubble had burst and the **chōnai** population was both shrinking and aging. To restore such a large float with such a complex shape seemed an incredible undertaking. In 2005, a friend of mine closely involved in the chōnai's efforts told me he thought it might take a hundred years to restore the float. "It costs 30 million yen[121] per year just to *maintain* a hoko," he explained.

---

[121] Approximately US$280,000 in May 2020.

The Restoration of Ōfune Boko

To the chōnai's enormous credit they brought it all together within a decade. Innovating with micro-donations, they invited the general public's support with a crowdfunding campaign,[122] for perhaps the first time in Gion Festival history. Donations accounted for more than 80 percent of the ¥120 million[123] in float restoration costs.

Surviving float treasures were displayed during the Gion Festival from 2007.

The reconstruction also became easier with other floats' support, university research, and technology. How so?

Ōfune Boko means the "Great Ship Float." It's a larger version of the **Fune Boko** ("Ship Float"). Both revere the semi-legendary, third-century Empress Jingū and three other deities who, legends say, ensured the success of her voyage to the Silla Kingdom (present-day Korean peninsula). In the **Saki Matsuri**, the Fune Boko is her ship on its way to Silla. The **Ato**

---

[122] While this is standard practice in places like North America, it was unusual in Japan at the time, particularly in the world of traditional Kyoto culture.

[123] Nearly US$1.2 million in July 2014, when **Ōfune Boko** rejoined the Gion Festival procession.

Matsuri's Ōfune Boko is her ship returning, bigger because it's full of tribute from Silla.[124]

While historic paintings and prints of **Ōfune Boko** existed, measurements did not. Fune Boko collaborated with Ritsumeikan University's Art Research Center to digitally measure their float's component parts and construction. These were scaled up to provide precise dimensions to reconstruct **Ōfune Boko**.

Ōfune Boko looked like this as recently as 2012, on display as part of the chōnai's fund development effort.

All of **Ōfune Boko's** sacred statues and regalia—except Empress Jingū's traditional **noh theater** mask and two of her kimono—were lost in the 1864 Great Genji Fire.[125] Some other treasures were saved and conserved, too, and decorate the newly reconstructed float. Each year every float strives to improve its decorations or presentation somehow. This may be most obvious with the newest floats—like **Ōfune Boko**—as year by year it commissions treasures to restore the float to glory.

---

[124] See **Fune Boko** for more on these deities and the legend of Empress Jingū.
[125] This gives us an idea of how precious these items were considered: people must have risked their lives to retrieve them.

A new sacred sculpture of Empress Jingū was the highest priority. In addition, historic paintings showed that a large dragon sculpture had adorned the boat's prow, but it had burned in the 1864 Great Genji Fire. Amazingly, research uncovered a duplicate sculpture in a Kyoto temple,[126] and this was used as a model to create the new one for **Ōfune Boko**.

*Ōfune Boko's newly carved dragon figurehead decorated its prow for the first time during the 2016 **Ato Matsuri** procession. During the 2016 Ato Matsuri, Ōfune Boko displayed the new dragon together with the 1804 sculpture it was modeled from.*

In a culture where the concept of "social impact" is still little known, the **Ōfune Boko** chōnai's social impact is exemplary. Among other things, residents worked together to save a traditional **kyōmachiya** townhouse from purchase by a real estate developer. Together they transformed it into their *kaisho* meeting place and treasure display area. **See Stepping into the Challenge** in the **Community** section for more.

---

[126] There's a history in Japan of creating duplicate artworks, so that artists and workshops could deliver commissioned goods even in case of disaster.

Suzuka Yama 鈴鹿山: The Demon-Pacifying Goddess

On the west side of Karasuma street, between Sanjō and Aneyakōji streets.

The Suzuka Yama float pays tribute to the goddess Suzuka Myōjin, protectress of Mt. Suzuka, a mountain peak between Mie and Shiga prefectures. Mt. Suzuka is located on the Tōkaidō road, the major route between Kyoto and Edo (now Tokyo). Its steep slopes were ideal for bandit raids, which became infamous. Over time the bandit raids morphed into tales of a terrible demon stalking travelers on Mt. Suzuka.

This float celebrates the legend that Suzuka—doubling as both a Shintō goddess and Buddhist saint—vanquished the demon. A red-haired "scalp" or wig representing the demon's head hangs from the pine tree's lowest branches. Kyoto commerce relied on trade via the Tōkaidō, so Suzuka was highly revered as a guardian of travelers and merchants.

The goddess Suzuka, protectress of travelers. Note the sakura-themed textile, ornate corner metalwork, and flaming jewels on wooden tablets in the pine tree.

In another version of the legend, Suzuka herself was the leader of a fearsome team of mountain bandits. To ensure safe trade and passage on the Tōkaidō, eighth-century Emperor Kammu sent his great shōgun Sakanoue no Tamuramaro to subdue them. Facing the beautiful Suzuka, Tamura invoked the name of his protectress, Kannon,[127] to help him be victorious. Knowing she was no match for Kannon, the bandit Suzuka laid down her weapons. She and Tamuramaro became a couple, and she became Lady Suzuka. Part of this story appears in the noh play Tamura, composed by the genius playwright Zeami.[128] It's also the subject of the Iwami Kagura[129] theater play, Suzuka Yama.

A small replica of Suzuka without a mask on Suzuka Yama's shrine to **Gozu Tennō**, *one of the Gion Festival's central deities. The offering vases are* bizen *ceramic.*

The noh mask worn by the sacred statue was carved in 1718, and indicates Suzuka's status as a goddess—her face beneath the mask is never revealed. Dressed in men's attire, wearing a sword at her

---

[127] You may recognize the bodhisattva of compassion from **Kita Kannon Yama** and **Minami Kannon Yama**. Tamuramaro also helped build Kyoto's famous Kiyomizu temple in the eighth century, and dedicated it to Kannon. Kiyomizu is highly worth a visit, particularly if you remember that it was built without a single nail. It's close to the Yasaka Pagoda of **Yamabushi Yama** fame.

[128] See **Ashikari Yama** for more on Zeami.

[129] See the **Dance and Music** section for information on Iwami Kagura at Yasaka Shrine during the Gion Festival.

THE GION FESTIVAL

waist, and wielding a *naginata*,[130] she also embodies Japan's female warrior or onna-bugeisha.

Note the unique wooden *e-ma* tablets—traditionally used for writing prayers at a temple or shrine—in Suzuka Yama's pine tree. These show a Shintō torii gate and mountains representing a shrine on Mt. Suzuka, or a flaming jewel, a Buddhist symbol for the enlightened mind. They're distributed after the July 24 procession as talismans, particularly against theft.

The renowned 20th-century textile artist Yamaga Seika lived in this **chōnai**: the ornate metalwork based on his designs depicts flora and fauna from the four seasons and decorates the float frame. One side-panel textile shows Japan's celebrated *sakura* cherry blossoms, while the other presents *momiji* autumn maples. Both are based on designs by the artist Imai Toshimitsu, who bridged 20th-century Japanese and European art.

A few doors south of the float's **kyōmachiya** meeting place is a family-run folding-fan shop, specializing

Girls greet visitors at the kaisho meeting place, backed by textiles and metalwork by world-class Japanese artists.

---

[130] The *naginata* (a sword-like blade on a pike or long pole) was traditionally a weapon used by women, as well as by sōhei warrior monks like **Benkei** and **Jōmyō**. One also decorates the top of **Naginata Boko's** central *shingi* pole.

in traditional fans for noh theater, dance, and Gion Festival's *ondotori* float "conductors." This family has long supported Suzuka Yama and Gion Festival traditions. You'll marvel at the artistry that goes into these beautiful fans.

Taka Yama 鷹山: The Falconry Float

On the north side of Sanjō street, east of Shinmachi street.

The Taka Yama **chōnai** is in the exciting process of restoring their float to the Gion Festival after an absence of nearly 200 years. While contemporary society and most urban cores suffer from disconnection, the Taka Yama chōnai is strengthening relationships within the neighborhood, with other Gion Festival chōnai, and with many other related organizations to succeed in their mission. We members of the public get to share the benefits.

*Taka Yama's sacred statues on display during the **Ato Matsuri**.*

Taka Yama's long Gion Festival history dates back at least to the 15th century. It started as a yama carried on men's shoulders, and burned in 1788's Great Tenmei Fire. By the early 1800s Taka Yama reappeared as a large, roofed yama pulled with ropes. A terrible storm struck during the 1826 Ato Matsuri procession and destroyed Taka Yama's decorations, preventing participation in subsequent processions. Then its float timbers burned in 1864's Great Genji Fire. The heads and hands of the sacred statues of its three deities were rescued, however, and the sacred statues were rebuilt. Since then, although Taka Yama itself has been absent, these sacred statues have been faithfully displayed during the Gion Festival.

This creation-destruction-re-creation cycle repeats throughout the Gion Festival's history. In a sense, the festival is all about the unceasing rhythms of life and death.

The three sacred statues portray a falconry hunting scene on an imperial outing with ninth-century Emperor Kōkō.[131] The main sacred statue shows the government official and poet Ariwara no Yukihara, an excellent falconer. He is accompanied by *Inu-kai*—literally, "dog-keeper"—and *Taru-oi*—the man with a barrel on his back and a *chimaki* in his hands. Presumably they both assisted in hunting.

Since the 2010s the local **chōnai** community has been well-occupied in its commitment to reintroduce Taka Yama into the Gion Festival procession. In 2012 it relaunched its ***ohayashi* musical troupe**. In 2017 Taka Yama gave public performances of the *gionbayashi* music with an impressive 48 musicians, and

The Taka Yama musicians and chōnai representatives taking part in the Ato Matsuri in 2019, the first time in 193 years.

the first *Hiyori Kagura* ritual[132] in 191 years. In 2019

---

[131] Emperor Kōkō revived a ceremonial tradition of imperial court falconry hunting in nearby Serikawa, along the northeast side of Lake Biwa in neighboring Shiga Prefecture. Lake Biwa is on the other side of the hills behind **Yasaka Shrine**.

[132] The night before the floats' procession, ohayashi musicians and float patrons walk to the otabisho for a ritual prayer

Taka Yama participated in the Ato Matsuri floats procession, with its ohayashi music troupe and a *karabitsu*, a box containing Taka Yama's sacred objects. The chōnai has been researching historical documents, paintings and prints, and raising funds with the goal of the Taka Yama float joining the Ato Matsuri procession in 2026, 200 years since it last participated.

While there's a tradition of competition among the chōnai for the best float, there's also a long tradition of collaboration. Other pulled *hiki-yama* floats are sharing their construction measurements and designs so that Taka Yama can determine how to rebuild its own float's frame. Since Taka Yama's own musical scores had been lost, they created a new melody based on neighboring **Kita Kannon Yama's**. In addition, Kyoto Municipal Arts University students have worked with the chōnai to develop costume designs. Textile and metalwork specialists are assisting with research to ascertain how to recreate the original Taka Yama's decorations.

Music performances during 2019's yoiyama included a multimedia display projected onto the wall behind the musicians.

Over the centuries numerous floats disappeared and have not recovered. So the newer floats indicate

---

to the main Yasaka Shrine/**Gion Festival deities** for good weather during the procession. They play music all the way.

the contemporary strength of their **chōnai's** community spirit, something to be proud of.

Falcon Float-themed merchandise helps raise funds to restore Taka Yama.

PRACTICAL TIPS

These tips will help make your Gion Festival experience more enjoyable. I learned all these things the hard way, and share them here so that you can have a more relaxed and pleasant time.

BEFORE YOU GO

- Kyoto is generally a very safe city.
- The festival is enormous, so it's not possible to do and see everything. That's okay. Relax and enjoy whatever unfolds for you.
- Keep in mind that this festival originated 1150+ years ago because of Kyoto's wet, hot (30-40 ℃ / 85-100 ℉), and humid (70 percent on average) mid-summer weather conditions. They're an integral part of the experience.
- The sun is strong—you'll be glad for a hat, sunscreen, and protective clothing.

*Offerings at a shrine in the **Abura Tenjin Yama** chōnai.*

- Kyotoites don't generally wear sunglasses, but if your eyes are sensitive you may want to.
- Visit the festival at the cooler times of the day and go somewhere air-conditioned (like one of Kyoto's numerous **museums**, shops, and Japanese restaurants/green tea houses) in the hottest hours of the day.
- Stay hydrated. Taking your own water bottle supports both the Gion Festival's fabulous Zero Waste campaign and our beautiful planet.

Beauty in so many forms. Decorative tassel, **Suzuka Yama**.

- Comfortable walking shoes or sandals that can get wet and slip on and off easily are your best friend.
- Prepare ultra-light rain gear (you will sweat) and a compact umbrella.
- A compass could come in handy.
- Carry petty cash (Japanese yen)—all the floats, festival food and game stalls, and some restaurants and shops are still cash-only.
  - Currency exchange is generally available only in major hotels and banks.

Beautiful woman textile, **Kakkyō Yama**, *based on a painting by* Uemura Shōkō.

- Inquire about acceptance of your particular ATM card before you leave your home country.
- At the time of writing, non-Japanese cellular data may or may not consistently work in Kyoto.
  - Consequently, some hotels provide a local smartphone with data. Others don't.
  - At the time of writing, I've tried a half dozen different methods over the years and still haven't found a way to get easy, reliable cellular data. This might help you enjoy being at the festival more.

Enjoying **Omukae Chōchin**.

- If attending the Saki Matsuri (July 12-17), visiting the southernmost and westernmost floats invites a less crowded and more community-oriented experience.
- The Ato Matsuri (July 20-24) is similarly more relaxed. Festival patrons tell me it is more like the Gion Festival used to be.
- Gion Festival crowds may help you redefine "crowded," particularly on July 16 and 17. Plan accordingly.
  - Particularly if traveling with children or people new to Kyoto, organize a rendezvous point and time as a Plan B; and

- Make sure everyone has your/their accommodation address and phone number (in Japanese too) on them as Plan C.
- Downtown traffic is very congested during the Gion Festival, so taxis, buses, and bicycles are not recommended.

- To get to the Gion Festival, the north-south subway line conveniently stops in the middle of it, at Shijō Karasuma (K 09).
  - The east-west Hankyu train line stops at the same station, called Shijō.
  - Oike Karasuma is convenient too, and both the north-south (K 08) and east-west (T 13) subway lines stop there.

ONCE YOU'RE THERE

- The logistical challenges of so many visitors in a country known for small spaces is considerable.
  - Accommodating visitors to the Gion Festival is almost entirely a volunteer undertaking, so our hosts deeply appreciate considerate guests.

Protector lion-dog guardian, **Yasaka Shrine.**

THE GION FESTIVAL

- Kyoto's ingenious feng shui urban planning makes it easy to stay well-oriented geographically.
  - Streets in central Kyoto are on north-south and east-west axes.
  - You can see the green *Higashiyama* Eastern Mountains behind **Yasaka Shrine** at the eastern end of Shijō street during the day.
- Take several rest breaks throughout the day. Then take more.

Dragon tassel holder, **Hōka Boko**.

- Drink Kyoto's delicious green tea for refreshment, caffeine without jitters, and health benefits. Wonderful to drink cold.
- The Gion Festival's ambitious Zero-Waste campaign includes an awesome recycling program run by enthusiastic youth. Being mindful of your waste is a great way to show your support for the sustainability of the festival and future generations.
- There are few public toilets outside the train station, so use restrooms when available.
  - Most convenience stores have them, and lines are long during the Gion Festival.
- Use a fan (men use them here too) and a handkerchief or small *tenugui* towel: they work well! There are

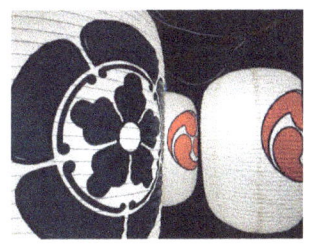

lots of fun ones for free and on sale around the festival.
- Buying a fan or towel from the *yamaboko* floats, particularly the smaller ones, helps support their economic health.
• As mentioned in the **Overview**, a Japanese proverb, *Ichigo, ichi-e,* translates roughly to: "This special moment, this unique coming together." It celebrates the extraordinariness of each moment, and how quickly the moment is gone forever. This kind of relaxed appreciation is still at the heart of the Gion Festival. Enjoy.

SCHEDULE

Please note that times, dates, and events in the festival schedule are subject to change. Note also that rituals are not designed to be tourist events, so access may be limited.

July 1

Kippu-iri: Each float neighborhood performs various rituals and meetings to launch the month of Gion Festival festivities. *Kura* storehouses are ritually opened, other ceremonies honor the float deities, and so on. These are not open to the public.

10:00: **Naginata Boko** *Chigo Shasan* Shrine Visit Naginata Boko float patrons and its **chigo** child (see 7/13) visit **Yasaka Shrine** to pray for the success of the festival this year. "Success" refers mainly to safety, health, and good weather for the July 17 procession.

July 2
Kippu-iri

10:00: *Kuji-tori*
Lots are chosen in this ceremony at City Hall to determine the order of floats in the processions, presided over by the mayor of Kyoto. (Some floats' positions are historically predetermined.)

11:30: **Yamaboko** *Shasan* Shrine Visit
Representatives of the various **chōnai** float neighborhoods visit **Yasaka Shrine** to pray for a safe and healthy festival, and for good weather.

July 3-5
Kippu-iri

July 7

14:30: **Ayagasa Boko** *Chigo Shasan* Shrine Visit
Patrons and **chigo** ceremonial children from the Ayagasa Boko float visit **Yasaka Shrine** to pray for the success of the festival this year.

July 10

Saki Matsuri begins.
This is the first half of the Gion Festival floats' activities, centering around the Shijō-Muromachi intersection.

Yama Boko Tate

From early morning, carpenters start the fascinating process of constructing some of the main Gion Festival floats. Visit throughout their progress and you'll never look at wood and rope in the same way again. On Shijō and Muromachi streets: **Kankō Boko**, **Kikusui Boko**, **Naginata Boko**, **Niwatori Boko**, **Tsuki Boko**. See **Maps** for float locations.

10:00: *Hei-Kiri*
Have you seen those paper zig-zags around? Those are waved to bless and purify a space, object, or person. In this ritual, **Yasaka Shrine** priests bless and cut such sacred paper implements used by members of the **Naginata Boko** float.

11:00 *Takabayashicho Shasan* Ritual at Yasaka Shrine Craftsmen from the Takabayashi-cho neighborhood visit **Yasaka Shrine** to bless the bamboo and rope they use to build the structure for the sacred rope-cutting that opens the **Saki Matsuri's yamaboko procession** on July 17, just west of Shijō-Fuyacho intersection. These craftsmen are similar to a guild, and have historically undertaken the honor of this construction.

13:00-17:00 (last entry 16:30): Tour the beautiful **Sugimoto family home** and enjoy its art treasures at **Hakuga Yama** to see how families and businesses flourished in this neighborhood over the last few hundred years. Supports its conservation. Adults:

¥1500 Children: ¥800. No photos. Confirm details on the Sugimoto-Ke website: en.sugimoto.or.jp.

16:30 *Omukae Chochin* (Welcoming Lanterns)
To prepare the city streets for tonight's **Mikoshi Arai** ritual, men, boys, and festival musicians dressed in kimono and yukata depart from **Yasaka Shrine** carrying paper lanterns. They walk along Shijō street to Kawaramachi street, then north to City Hall. They're followed by a procession of children dressed in colorful costumes, some of whom will reappear in the **Hanagasa Junkō** on July 24. In the middle of this Omukae Chochin procession, they perform children's dances at City Hall.

17:30 Children's Dances at City Hall
Children perform three kinds of dance: a *Sagi Mai* heron dance, *Komachi Odori* (beautiful young woman's dance), and the Gion Matsuri Ondō. Then they continue walking south along Teramachi to Shijō, then back to **Yasaka Shrine**, where a second dance performance is given when the mikoshi returns from *mikoshi arai*, around 20:45.

19:00: *Mikoshi Arai*: Portable Shrine Ritual Cleansing
Purification ritual for **Yasaka Shrine**'s portable *mikoshi* shrines. Shrine parishioners carry the *mikoshi*, leaving Yasaka Shrine at 19:00. They arrive at Shijō Bridge (at Kawabata street, over the Kamo River) for a purification ritual at 20:00. They carry them back to Yasaka Shrine, arriving around 20:45.

On their return, the children mentioned above (in the City Hall dances at 17:30) perform lovely dances.

July 11
Saki Matsuri

Yama Boko Tate
Carpenters continue to build Gion Festival floats on Shijō street and on Shinmachi street. Their rope-tying skills will astound you. It's for safety, strength, flexibility, and beauty. See **Maps** for float locations.

13:00-17:00 (last entry 16:30): Tour the beautiful **Sugimoto family home** and enjoy its art treasures at **Hakuga Yama** to see how families and businesses flourished in this neighborhood over the last few hundred years. Support its conservation. Adults: ¥1500 Children: ¥800. No photos. Confirm details on the Sugimoto-Ke website: en.sugimoto.or.jp.

July 12
Saki Matsuri

A.M.: *Yama Boko Tate*
Float carpenters and staff continue building and decorating the yamaboko floats. See **Maps** for float locations.

13:00-17:00 (last entry 16:30): Tour the beautiful **Sugimoto family home** and enjoy its art treasures at **Hakuga Yama**, to see how families and businesses have flourished in this neighborhood over the last few hundred years. The fee supports its conservation. Adults: ¥1500 Children: ¥800. No photos. Confirm details on the Sugimoto-Ke website: en.sugimoto.or.jp.

14:00-15:45: *Hoko Hikizome*
Floats on Shijō street and Muromachi street do a test pull, with musicians playing **music**, to make sure the hoko have been constructed properly. Anyone from the public can join in the pulling. Be very careful. Begins with **Kankō Boko**, then **Niwatori Boko**, **Kikusui Boko**, **Tsuki Boko**, and **Naginata Boko**. Prepare for crowds.

P.M. Lanterns hung for larger hoko floats.

18:00 **Gionbayashi music** begins with **Kankō Boko** and **Kikusui Boko**, just west of the Shijō-Karasuma intersection. See **Maps** for float locations.

July 13
Saki Matsuri

Yama Boko Tate – Float construction and decoration continue. See **Maps** for float locations.

A.M.: **Fune Boko** gets decorated.

11:00: *Chigo Shasan*
Naginata Boko's **chigo** child visits **Yasaka Shrine**. The *chigo-san* is an ancient Gion Festival tradition;

a boy from a prominent Kyoto family is chosen to represent a medium for the **festival deity**. In this ceremony, he's led on horseback to Yasaka Shrine for ritual prayers for the safety of the festival procession on July 17.

14:00: Sacred *chigo* child ceremony at **Yasaka Shrine**
The two Kuze koma-gata-chigo—children chosen from southern Kyoto's Kuze neighborhood to accompany Yasaka Shrine's portable **mikoshi** shrines in the **Shinkōsai** and **Kankōsai**—participate in a ritual at Yasaka Shrine. This ritual is not designed for tourists, so catching any glimpses of it is good fortune.

15:00: *Yamaboko Hikizome* (Floats test pull)
Floats on Shinmachi street do a test pull, with musicians playing **music**, to make sure the floats have been constructed properly. Anyone from the public can join in the pulling. **Iwatō Yama**, **Fune Boko**, **Hōka Boko**. Expect crowds and be careful. Afterward (around 16:00) at **Iwatō Yama**, local school children perform a cute (nontraditional) dance to a specially arranged *gionbayashi* **music** tune. See **Maps** for float locations.

13:00-21:00: Enjoy tea ceremony at **Kikusui Boko** and take home a lovely souvenir dish for ¥2000.

18:00~> **Gionbayashi music** on Shijō, Muromachi, and Shinmachi streets.

July 14
Saki Matsuri

Yama Tate
Construction of all the large **yamaboko** is complete, but the numerous smaller Saki Matsuri yama continue to be constructed and decorated.

By today all of the yamaboko floats' shrines celebrating their respective deities and displaying their treasures will be open to the public. Look closely, as it's a rare opportunity to see priceless art without glass or space between you. Resist the urge to touch so we can continue to enjoy the treasures in this extraordinary way for years to come. See the pages on each **float** to learn more. See **Maps** for float locations.

Byōbu Matsuri
Local families and businesses display their historic treasures for the public to enjoy. Acting like an honored guest in their home will help ensure that the tradition continues.

10:00-20:00 (last entry 19:30) Visit **Nagae-Ke**, the traditional Nagae family residence, to see what kimono businesses and homes were like in years gone by. Kyoto has few conservation laws for such traditional buildings, and this one was recently purchased by a real estate developer. If you appreciate their effort to conserve this historic building, it might be helpful to let them know. In front of

THE GION FESTIVAL

Fune Boko. Adults: ¥700 High school students: ¥600 Younger children: ¥300.

12:00-21:00 Enjoy tea ceremony at **Kikusui Boko**, and take home a souvenir tea dish, for ¥2000.

16:30-21:00 (last entry 20:30): Tour the beautiful **Sugimoto family home** and enjoy a new grouping of art treasures—*all changed the day before*—at **Hakuga Yama**, to see how families and businesses have flourished in this neighborhood over the last few hundred years. The fee supports its conservation. Adults: ¥1500 Children: ¥800. No photos. Confirm details on the Sugimoto-Ke website: en.sugimoto.or.jp.

Yoiyoiyoiyama

Festival highlight. Three "yois" mean three nights before the procession on the 17th. All floats' shrine areas celebrating their respective deities and displaying their treasures are open and all musical troupes play music until 21:00-22:00, centered near the Shijō-Karasuma intersection, Shijō station on the north-south subway line and Hankyu train line. You can also easily walk from Oike Karasuma subway stations. See **Maps** for float locations.

18:00 and 19:00: Shintō-style dance and music by professional performers at **Iwatō Yama**. It's not a part of the Gion Festival tradition, but lovely. In case of rain, it will be held indoors (limited space available). Expect crowds.

18:40-22:20: **Ayagasa Boko**'s energetic music starts at 18:40 and every hour at the same time thereafter, including 21:40. Its remarkable *bō-furi* stick-whirling dance takes place every hour from 19:00 through and including 22:00. Performances 20 minutes each. *Visit **Ayagasa Boko**'s location to confirm this year's posted timetable.* Expect crowds.

19:00~> Enjoy **Shijō Kasa Boko**'s music performances every 40 minutes through and including 21:00. They perform in the street so you can get a good view. *Visit **Shijō Kasa Boko**'s location to confirm this year's posted timetable.*

July 15
Saki Matsuri

10:00~> Most floats' shrines celebrating their respective deities and displaying their treasures are open from 10:00 until 21:00-22:00 on this night. See **Maps** for float locations.

Byōbu Matsuri (Folding Screen Festival)
Local families and businesses display their historic treasures for the public to enjoy. Expressing our appreciation may help keep them motivated to continue sharing in this way.

11:00~> *Yamabushi* (ascetic nature-mystic monks) chant the *Heart Sutra* at **Yamabushi Yama** to pay respects to renowned ninth-century yamabushi Jōzō Kisho, celebrated there. Followed by a fire ritual for world peace. Times subject to change. Prepare for crowds.

10:00-20:00 (last entry 19:30): Visit **Nagae-Ke**, the traditional Nagae family residence, to see what kimono businesses and homes were like in years gone by. Kyoto has few conservation laws for such traditional buildings, and this one was recently purchased by a real estate developer. If you appreciate their effort to conserve this historic building, it may be helpful to let them know. In front of **Fune Boko**. Adults: ¥700 High school students: ¥600 Younger children: ¥300.

10:30-21:00 (last entry 20:30): Tour the beautiful **Sugimoto family home** and enjoy their exquisite art treasures at **Hakuga Yama**, to see how families and businesses have flourished in this neighborhood over the last few hundred years. Supports its conservation. Adults: ¥1500 Children: ¥800. No photos. Confirm details on the Sugimoto-Ke website: en.sugimoto.or.jp.

13:00-22:00 Enjoy tea ceremony at **Kikusui Boko**, and take home a souvenir tea dish, for ¥2000.

14:30: **Naginata Boko**'s *chigo* child practices with a real sword for the sacred rope-cutting ceremony that opens the July 17 procession. At Naginata Boko.

***Yoiyoiyama*:**
Festival highlight. Two "yois" mean two more nights before the processions on July 17. All floats' shrine areas celebrating their respective deities and displaying their treasures are open and all musical troupes play **music** until 21:00-22:00, centered near the Shijō-Karasuma intersection, Shijō station on the north-south subway line and Hankyu train line. You can also easily walk from Oike Karasuma subway stations. See **Maps** for float locations.

18:00-23:00: Central Kyoto roads are closed to traffic for the Gion Festival, transformed into "Pedestrian Paradise" (that's what the signs call it). Parameters are generally from **Yasaka Shrine** in the east all the way to Horikawa street in the west and from Takatsuji street (three blocks south of Shijō) in the south to Oike street in the north. This area is subject to change by Kyoto City. Be prepared for tremendous crowds.

18:00: Children's *Warabe-Mai*, *Kami Asobi* (God-Pleasing) Dance, **Iwatō Yama**. Local school children join in the festival spirit with a group dance to their float's festival music.

18:40-22:20: **Ayagasa Boko**'s energetic music starts at 18:40 and every hour at the same time thereafter, including 21:40. Its remarkable *bō-furi* stick-whirling dance takes place every hour from 19:00 through and including 22:00. Performances

20 minutes each. *Visit **Ayagasa Boko**'s location to confirm this year's posted timetable.* Expect crowds.

19:00~> Enjoy **Shijō Kasa Boko**'s stick-whirling dance by children, together with music performances, every 40 minutes through and including 21:00. They also rehearse the graceful *Kuji Aratame*, when a float representative shows the float's numbered position in the procession to the mayor on July 17. They perform in the street so you can get a good view. *Visit **Shijō Kasa Boko**'s location to confirm this year's posted timetable.*

20:00: *Mitama-Utsushi* ("Spirit transfer"), **Yasaka Shrine**. The three main deities revered at Yasaka Shrine and in the Gion Festival are conveyed from their usual abode inside the main *honden* hall into the three portable *mikoshi* shrines. The entire shrine is darkened for this ritual. Expect crowds.

July 16
Saki Matsuri

Pay respects to the **Yasaka Shrine deities** and admire their **mikoshi** portable shrines on display at Yasaka Shrine's central stage.

10:00~> Most floats' treasure display areas open from 10:00 until 21:00-22:00 on this night. See **Maps** for float locations.

Byōbu Matsuri (Folding Screen Festival)
Local families and businesses display their historic treasures for the public to enjoy.

10:00-20:00 (last entry 19:30): Visit **Nagae-Ke**, the traditional Nagae family residence, to see what kimono businesses and homes were like in years gone by. Kyoto has few conservation laws for such traditional buildings, and this one was recently purchased by a real estate developer. If you appreciate their effort to conserve this historic building, it may be helpful to let them know. In front of **Fune Boko**. Adults: ¥700 High school students: ¥600 Younger children: ¥300.

10:30-21:00 (last entry 20:30): Tour the beautiful **Sugimoto family home** and enjoy their exquisite art treasures at **Hakuga Yama**, to see how families and businesses have flourished in this neighborhood over the last few hundred years. Supports its conservation. Adults: ¥1500 Children: ¥800. No photos. Confirm details on the Sugimoto-Ke website: en.sugimoto.or.jp.

12:00-22:00: Enjoy tea ceremony at **Kikusui Boko**, and take home a souvenir tea dish, for ¥2000.

Yoiyama:
Festival highlight. One "yoi" means one more night before the processions on July 17. All floats' shrine areas celebrating their respective deities and displaying their treasures are open and all musical troupes

play music until 21:00-22:00, centered near the Shijō-Karasuma intersection, Shijō station on the north-south subway line and Hankyu train line. You can also easily walk from Oike Karasuma subway stations. See **Maps** for float locations.

18:00-23:00: Central Kyoto roads are closed to traffic for the Gion Festival, transformed into "Pedestrian Paradise" (that's what the signs call it). Parameters are generally from Yasaka Shrine in the east all the way to Horikawa street in the west and from Takatsuji street (three blocks south of Shijō) in the south to Oike street in the north. This area is subject to change by Kyoto City. Be prepared for tremendous crowds.

18:00 Festival eve, celebrating to please the gods, **Yasaka Shrine**.
There are various events inside Yasaka Shrine and on Shijō street at the shrine entrance, preparing for the Gion Festival deities' journey downtown tomorrow. Subject to change yearly, events may include things like dance, theater, and taiko drums. There are food and other street stalls inside Yasaka Shrine also.

18:10-20:30: **Ayagasa Boko**'s energetic music starts at 18:10 and every hour at the same time thereafter including 20:10. Its remarkable *bō-furi* stick-whirling dance takes place once an hour starting at 18:30 through and including 20:30. Performances 20 minutes each. *Visit Ayagasa Boko's location to confirm this year's posted timetable.* Expect crowds.

18:30-21:00: *Iwami Kagura* dance theater, **Yasaka Shrine**
This spectacular Chinese-style dance is performed to please the gods. People get to enjoy it as well. These dances change yearly and celebrate various deities revered in the Gion Festival. Expect crowds.

19:00~> Enjoy **Shijō Kasa Boko**'s stick-whirling dance by children, together with music performances, every 40 minutes through and including 21:00. They also rehearse the graceful *Kuji Aratame*, when a float representative shows the float's numbered position in the procession to the mayor on July 17. They perform in the street so you can get a good view.

21:00-23:00: *Hiyori Kagura* ("Good Weather Music for the Deities")
Float musicians and patrons walk from their floats to the *otabisho** "visiting place" (only Naginata Boko musicians and patrons walk all the way to Yasaka Shrine and back, from 22:00), playing festival music and wearing festival dress, to pray for good weather for the procession on July 17.

*Located on the southeast side of the Shijō-Teramachi intersection, the otabisho is where the Yasaka Shrine deities will visit downtown Kyoto in their portable **mikoshi** shrines. They stay at the otabisho from the night of July 17 until the night of July 24, when they're returned to Yasaka Shrine.

THE GION FESTIVAL

July 17
Saki Matsuri

Pay respects to the **Yasaka Shrine deities** and admire their **mikoshi** portable shrines on display at Yasaka Shrine's central stage.

8:00-12:30: *Yamabako Junkō* **Floats Procession**
Floats prepare to depart from Shijō-Karasuma intersection from around 9:00 for the grand Saki Matsuri *Yamaboko Junko* or float procession. If you wait to enjoy the later floats, the crowds thin. Prepare for crowds and heat. See **Maps** for the route.

9:00: *Shimenawa-Kiri* Ceremony
Naginata Boko's **chigo**-san cuts the sacred rope west of the Shijō-Fuyacho intersection, thereby opening the sacred space of the festival procession. Extremely crowded.

9:00~> *Kuji-aratame*: Floats procession order confirmation
The order of the floats is confirmed with a graceful, ritual presentation of the floats' numbered place in the procession on Shijō street at Sakaimachi street.

9:40~> Floats travel down Shijō street to Kawaramachi street (9:40-11:40), north to Oike street (10:30-12:30), west to Shinmachi street (11:30-13:15), then south again, returning to their respective neighborhoods. See **Maps**.

Turning the larger yamaboko floats at the corners—called **Tsuji Mawashi**—is an amazing and popular spectacle, as the giant wheels do not turn. Prepare for crowds and heat.

12:30~> After the procession, the yamaboko are dismantled. It's remarkable to watch this giant mandala dissolve. The larger hoko take down their textiles and other treasures, but leave the roof on until the timbers are taken down on July 18.

16:00: Sacred *chigo* child ceremony at **Yasaka Shrine**
There are two *Kuze koma-gata-chigo*, ceremonial children chosen from southern Kyoto's Kuze neighborhood to accompany Yasaka Shrine's portable **mikoshi** shrines in the **Shinkōsai** this night and in the **Kankōsai** on July 24. They participate in a ritual at Yasaka Shrine. This ritual is not designed for tourists, so catching any glimpses of it is good fortune.

16:00-22:00: **Shinkōsai** (神幸祭)
The Yasaka Shrine deities are transported in portable **mikoshi** shrines on the shoulders of hundreds of shouting men, blessing the streets of central Kyoto along the way. Various rituals take place from 16:00 at Yasaka Shrine. The mikoshi depart from the Yasaka Shrine front steps from 17:30. Each of three mikoshi takes a different route to finally arrive at the *otabisho* "visiting place" at the Shijō-Teramachi intersection. Follow along when the procession departs from Yasaka Shrine. If you miss that, all three travel south on Kawaramachi street from Sanjō street to Shijō

street, heading west there between 20:00-22:00 to end at the otabisho "visiting place" on Shijō at Teramachi street from 20:30-22:30. Access an interactive map of the mikoshi routes at GionFestival.org.

July 18
Saki Matsuri

Pay respects to the **Yasaka Shrine** deities and admire their **mikoshi** portable shrines on display at the otabisho visiting place on the southeast side of Shijō Teramachi intersection (see **Maps**).

The larger hoko floats continue to be dismantled, dissolving the annual mandala.

Ato Matsuri begins.

The Ato Matsuri is smaller and more intimate than the Saki Matsuri. With fewer crowds and a more community feeling, it's reminiscent of the Gion Festival of years gone by.

A.M.: **Ōfune Boko** construction begins.

July 19
Ato Matsuri

Pay respects to the **Yasaka Shrine** deities and admire their **mikoshi** portable shrines on display at the otabisho visiting place on the southeast side of Shijō Teramachi intersection (see **Maps**).

Yamaboko Tate (float construction)
A.M.: **Minami Kannon Yama**, **Kita Kannon Yama**, **Koi Yama** construction begins. See **Maps** for float locations.

July 20
Ato Matsuri

Pay respects to the **Yasaka Shrine** deities and admire their **mikoshi** portable shrines on display at the otabisho visiting place on the southeast side of Shijō Teramachi intersection (see **Maps**).

Yamaboko Tate (float construction)
A.M.: **Hashi Benkei Yama**, **Hachiman Yama**, **Kuronushi Yama**, **Jyōmyō Yama**, **En-no-Gyōja Yama**, **Suzuka Yama** construction begins. See **Maps** for float locations.

14:30: **Hikizome** float test pull
Test pull of **Ōfune Boko**, **Minami Kannon Yama**, and **Kita Kannon Yama** on Shinmachi street, south and north of Shijō. They get pulled simultaneously, so you have to choose one. Anyone can participate. Be careful. Arrive early and expect crowds. See **Maps** for float locations.

July 21
Ato Matsuri

Pay respects to the **Yasaka Shrine** deities and admire their **mikoshi** portable shrines on display at the otabisho visiting place on the southeast side of Shijō Teramachi intersection (see **Maps**).

9:00: **Hashi Benkei Yama** *kakizome* float test run
Hashi Benkei Yama is the only kaki-yama (a yama carried on the shoulders, rather than pulled by ropes) to do a test run, and the amazing chōnai members do it themselves. They go east then west along Takoyakushi street, beginning just west of Karasuma street.

10:00~> Larger floats' shrine areas celebrating their respective deities and displaying their treasures are open from the morning, and smaller floats set up their treasure displays today and open in the evening. Open until 21:00-22:00 on this night. See **Maps** for float locations.

Byōbu Matsuri (Folding Screen Festival)
Local families and businesses display their historic treasures for the public to enjoy. Festival patrons on Shinmachi street north of Takoyakushi street share particularly generously. Acting like an honored guest at their homes helps ensure that the tradition continues.

13:00-18:00 (last entry 17:30): Tour the beautiful **Sugimoto family home** and enjoy a *new grouping* of their exquisite art treasures—*changed since the Saki Matsuri*—at **Hakuga Yama**, to see how families and businesses have flourished in this neighborhood over the last few hundred years. Supports its conservation. Adults: ¥1500 Children: ¥800. No photos. Confirm details on the Sugimoto-Ke website: en.sugimoto.or.jp.

P.M.: Tonight is known as *Yoiyoiyoiyama*; three "yois" mean three nights before the procession on the 24th. All floats' shrine areas celebrating their respective deities and displaying their treasures are open. (Worth visiting! Near the floats look for paper lanterns in front of a small door, with rope and white paper zig-zags overhead.) Musical troupes play at **Ōfune Boko**, **Minami Kannon Yama**, and **Kita Kannon Yama** on Shinmachi street, plus at **Taka Yama** on Sanjō street. You can easily walk from Shijō station on the north-south subway line and Hankyu train line, and from Oike Karasuma subway stations. See **Maps** for float locations.

July 22
Ato Matsuri

Pay respects to the **Yasaka Shrine** deities and admire their **mikoshi** portable shrines on display at the otabisho visiting place on the southeast side of Shijō Teramachi intersection (see **Maps**).

10:00~> Most floats' shrine areas celebrating their respective deities and displaying their treasures are open from 10:00 until 21:00-22:00. See **Maps** for float locations.

Worth visiting! Near the floats, look for paper lanterns in front of a small door, with rope and white paper zig-zags overhead.

Byōbu Matsuri (Folding Screen Festival)
Local families and businesses display their historic treasures for the public to enjoy. Festival patrons on Shinmachi street north of Takoyakushi street share particularly generously.

13:00-18:00 (last entry 17:30): Tour the beautiful **Sugimoto family home** and enjoy a *new grouping* of their exquisite art treasures—*changed since the Saki Matsuri*—at **Hakuga Yama**, to see how families and businesses have flourished in this neighborhood over the last few hundred years. Your visit supports its conservation. Adults: ¥1500 Children: ¥800. No photos. Confirm details on the Sugimoto-Ke website: en.sugimoto.or.jp.

P.M.: Yoiyoiyama
Two "yois" mean two more nights before the procession on the 24th. All floats' shrine areas celebrating their respective deities and displaying their treasures are open for visiting. Musical troupes play at **Ōfune Boko**, **Minami Kannon Yama**, and **Kita Kannon Yama** on Shinmachi street, plus at **Taka Yama** on Sanjō street. You can easily walk from Shijō station on the north-south subway line and Hankyu train line, and from Oike Karasuma subway stations. See **Maps** for float locations.

July 23
Ato Matsuri

Pay respects to the **Yasaka Shrine** deities and admire their **mikoshi** portable shrines on display at the otabisho visiting place on the southeast side of Shijō Teramachi intersection (see **Maps**).

9:00: *Kencha-sai* Ritual Tea Ceremony
Tea ceremony is performed by the heads of Kyoto tea ceremony schools at **Yasaka Shrine**.

10:00~> Most floats' shrine areas celebrating their respective deities and displaying their treasures are open from 10:00 until 21:00-22:00. See **Maps** for float locations.

Byōbu Matsuri (Folding Screen Festival)
Local families and businesses display their historic treasures for the public to enjoy. Festival patrons on Shinmachi street north of Takoyakushi street share particularly generously.

13:00-18:00 (last entry 17:30): Tour the beautiful **Sugimoto family home** and enjoy a *new grouping* of their exquisite art treasures—*changed since the Saki Matsuri*—at **Hakuga Yama**, to see how families and businesses have flourished in this neighborhood over the last few hundred years. Our entry fees support its conservation. Adults: ¥1500 Children: ¥800. No photos. Confirm details on the Sugimoto-Ke website: en.sugimoto.or.jp.

THE GION FESTIVAL

13:00: Biwa performance at **Yasaka Shrine**
The *biwa* or Japanese lute is related to China's *pipa* instrument, and features a distinctive sound. Legend holds that it's the instrument of choice for Benzaiten—the Japanese goddess of the arts, learning, and love—the Japanese version of Sarasvati.

14:15 Ascetic *yamabushi* chant while ritually burning prayers written on fragrant wooden sticks in a sacred fire ritual at **En-no-Gyōja Yama**. Expect crowds. Lasts about one hour.

P.M.: Yoiyama
The night before the procession on the 24th. All floats' shrine areas celebrating their respective deities and displaying their treasures are open (worth visiting! Look for a small door with a rope and white paper zig-zags overhead). Musical troupes play at **Ōfune Boko**, **Minami Kannon Yama**, and **Kita Kannon Yama** on Shinmachi street, plus at **Taka Yama** on Sanjō street. Be prepared for crowds. You can easily walk from Shijō station on the north-south subway line and Hankyu train line, and from Oike Karasuma subway stations. See **Maps** for float locations.

18:00~> **Ōfune Boko** plays its gionbayashi **music** for 20 minutes then takes a 20-minute break, all night. Start times: 18:00, 18:40, 19:20, 20:00, 20:40, then 21:10. Please confirm times at **Ōfune Boko**.

21:30-23:00, *Hiyori Kagura ("Good Weather Music for the Deities")*.
Ōfune Boko, **Minami Kannon Yama**, **Kita Kannon Yama**, and **Taka Yama** patrons and *ohayashi* musicians walk and play *gionbayashi* **music** to and back from the otabisho at the Shijō-Teramachi intersection, to pray to the **Yasaka Shrine deities** for good weather for the procession tomorrow. Times and routes vary. **Ōfune Boko**'s ohayashi music troupe goes from its **kaisho** meeting place, up Shinmachi street to Sanjō street, east to the Teramachi arcade, then south to the otabisho on Shijō. It returns directly along Shijō and back to its *kaisho* home on Shinmachi street.

23:00 *Abare Kannon*
Minami Kannon Yama's precious statue of Kannon, the Buddhist bodhisattva of compassion, is carried boisterously around the neighborhood to spread blessings of compassion. It's wrapped in fabric so only the shape is barely visible above people's heads. Prepare for crowds.

July 24
Ato Matsuri

Pay respects to the **Yasaka Shrine** deities and admire their **mikoshi** portable shrines on display at the otabisho visiting place on the southeast side of Shijō Teramachi intersection (see **Maps**).

THE GION FESTIVAL

9:00: *Ato Matsuri* **Yamaboko Junkō Floats Procession**
The 11 floats in the Ato Matsuri line up to begin the procession from the Oike-Karasuma intersection, preparing to depart at 9:30.

They travel east to Kawaramachi street (10:10), south to Shijō street (10:45), and west to Karasuma street (11:20), then return to their respective neighborhoods. See **Maps** for the route.
Arrive early and prepare for crowds.

10:00: **Hanagasa Junkō** *(Flower Umbrella Procession)*
If you're a fan of **performing arts**, geiko-san—apprenticing maiko and master geisha—and children, this procession and its subsequent performances are for you. Ten large umbrellas accompanied by more than 500 people leave **Yasaka Shrine**'s front steps at 10:00, go west on Shijō street, turn north on the Teramachi arcade (10:30), and turn east again on Oike street (10:50) to Kyoto City Hall. They continue briefly to the east on Oike street, turning south on Kawaramachi street (11:10) until they arrive at Shijō street (11:20) and turn east again. They travel east back to Yasaka Shrine once more, arriving around noon. On their arrival traditional dance and music, including the Sagi Mai heron dance, are performed at the Shrine, ending around 17:30. See **Maps** for the route. Arrive early and prepare for crowds.

16:30: ***Kankōsai***: Portable **mikoshi** shrines return to **Yasaka Shrine**.
This is the lively return trip of the **Shinkōsai** we saw on July 17. There are three processions, one for each of three mikoshi. Each one takes a different route, so it's easiest to follow along when the procession departs from the vicinity of the *otabisho* near the Shijō-Teramachi intersection. They depart from the otabisho at staggered times between 16:30 and 18:15. If you miss that, all three go east on Sanjō street between 20:00-21:00, then south on the Teramachi arcade on their way to Shijō street, then due east to return to Yasaka Jinja. All mikoshi return to Yasaka Shrine between 22:00 and 23:00. Access an interactive map of the mikoshi routes at GionFestival.org to better enjoy the raucousness along the way.

21:00 Sacred ***chigo*** child ceremony at **Yasaka Shrine**
There are two *Kuze koma-gata-chigo,* ceremonial children chosen from southern Kyoto's Kuze neighborhood to accompany Yasaka Shrine's portable **mikoshi** shrines in the **Shinkōsai** on July 17 and the **Kankōsai** this night. They participate in a closing ritual at Yasaka Shrine. This ritual is not designed for tourists, so catching any glimpses of it is good fortune.

23:00-00:00: *Mitama-utsushi* ("Spirit transfer"), **Yasaka Shrine**. The three main deities revered at Yasaka Shrine and in the Gion Festival are conveyed from the three portable mikoshi shrines back to their usual abode inside the main *honden* hall.

Takes place shortly after the deities/mikoshi are returned to Yasaka Shrine by hundreds of men in the kankōsai processions. The entire shrine is darkened for this ritual. This is an intimate ritual attended by a lot of people, rather than a tourist event. Expect crowds.

July 25

11:00 or 13:00 *Kyōgen* Traditional Comic Theater
A traditional performance by the famed Shigeyama family school, on the Yasaka Shrine noh stage. Because it's comedy, kyōgen is fairly easy to enjoy even when we don't understand the narrative.

July 28

10:00: Water Blessing Ceremony.
The water is scooped from the Kamo River and blessed in a ritual so that it's ready to be used in the **Mikoshi Arai** ceremony tonight. In between, it's kept at a small shrine on the southeast side of the Shijō bridge, along Kamo River.

19:00: ***Mikoshi Arai***: Portable Shrine Ritual Cleansing
Accompanied by the purifying fires of giant torches, **Yasaka Shrine** parishioners carry **mikoshi** by procession to the middle of the Shijō Bridge. At 20:00 they're cleansed with ritually blessed water gathered earlier from the Kamogawa River. Yasaka Shrine parishioners carry the mikoshi back to Yasaka Shrine, arriving around 20:45.

July 31

10:00: *Eki Jinja Nagoshi-Sai:* Epidemic-Banishing Closing Ritual of Gion Festival.

This purification ceremony signifies the Gion Festival's completion and recalls the commitment made by the god of storms and **Yasaka Shrine deity** Susano-o-no-Mikoto to Somin Shōrai, the humble man who generously gave him shelter (see **History**). You too can stand in line to pass through a large *chi no wa* straw hoop at the torii gate entryway to the *Eki Jinja* or "Epidemic Shrine," within Yasaka Shrine. This purifies body, mind, and spirit, protecting from malevolence for the year. Rebirth symbolism abounds.

Please note that times, dates, and events in the festival schedule are subject to change. Note also that rituals are not designed to be tourist events, so visibility may be limited.

MAPS

YASAKA SHRINE SITES

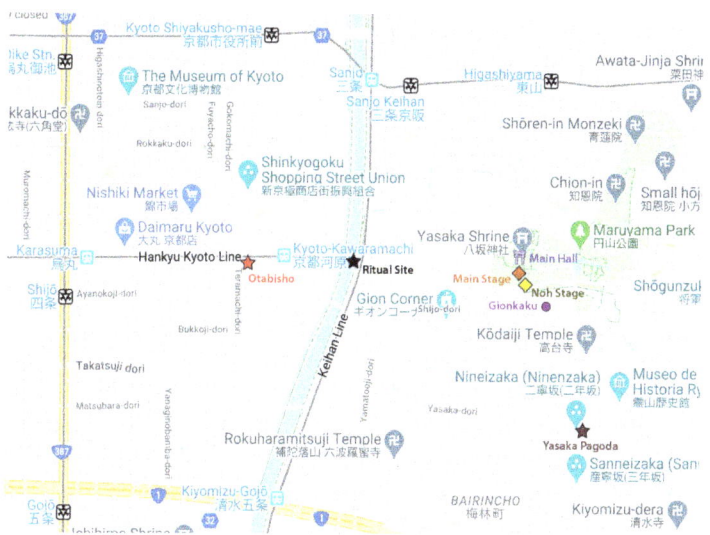

YASAKA SHRINE SITES

- ⭐ 7/17-24 Otabisho
  (On the SW corner of Shijo and Teramachi streets)
- ★ 7/10 & 7/28 Mikoshi Arai––
  Portable Shrine Purification Ritual
- ⛩ Main Hall (honden)
- ◆ Main Stage (Mikoshi / Dance)
- ◇ Noh Stage
- ★ Yasaka Pagoda
- ● Gionkaku (Dōkaku) hoko shaped hall

"Street" is *dori* in Japanese.

Created by Catherine Pawasarat and Google Maps

Please visit GionFestival.org for my interactive maps.

Festival Floats (saki matsuri)

Saki Matsuri Floats' Locations

☆ Boardable
◇ Boardable (men only)

- 01-Abura Tenjin Yama
- 02-Arare Tenjin Yama
- 03-Ashikari Yama
- 04-Ayagasa Boko
- 05-Fune Boko
- 06-Hakuga Yama
- 07-Hakurakuten Yama
- 08-Hōka Boko
- 09-Hoshō Yama
- 10-Iwatō Yama
- 11-Kakkyō Yama
- 12-Kankō Boko
- 13-Kikusui Boko
- 14-Mōsō Yama
- 15-Naginata Boko
- 16-Niwatori Boko
- 17-Shijo Kasa Boko
- 18-Taishi Yama
- 19-Tokusa Yama
- 20-Tōrō Yama
- 21-Tsuki Boko
- 22-Urade Yama
- 23-Yamabushi Yama

"Street" is *dori* in Japanese.

Created by Catherine Pawasarat and Google Maps
Please visit GionFestival.org for my interactive maps.

Saki Matsuri Procession (7/17)

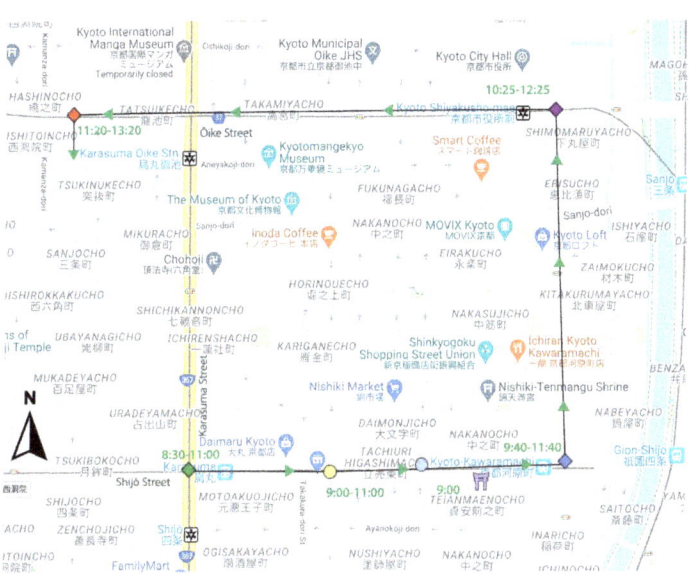

🛕 Otabisho

◆ 8:30-11:00 Floats gather & start on Shijō street, between Nishinotoin and Karasuma streets.

○ 9:00 Shimenawa-kiri rope-cutting, Fuyachō-Shijō intersection.

○ 9:00-11:00 Kuji Aratame ritual, Sakaimachi-Shijō.

◆ 9:40-11:40 Tsuji Mawashi, Kawaramachi-Shijō intersection.

◆ 10:25-12:25 Tsuji Mawashi, Kawaramachi-Oike intersection.

◆ 11:20-13:20 Final Tsuji Mawashi & Procession End, Shinmachi-Oike intersection.

Route goes counterclockwise. Times approximate.

"Street" is *dori* in Japanese.

Created by Catherine Pawasarat and Google Maps
Please visit GionFestival.org for my interactive maps.

Festival Floats (Ato Matsuri)

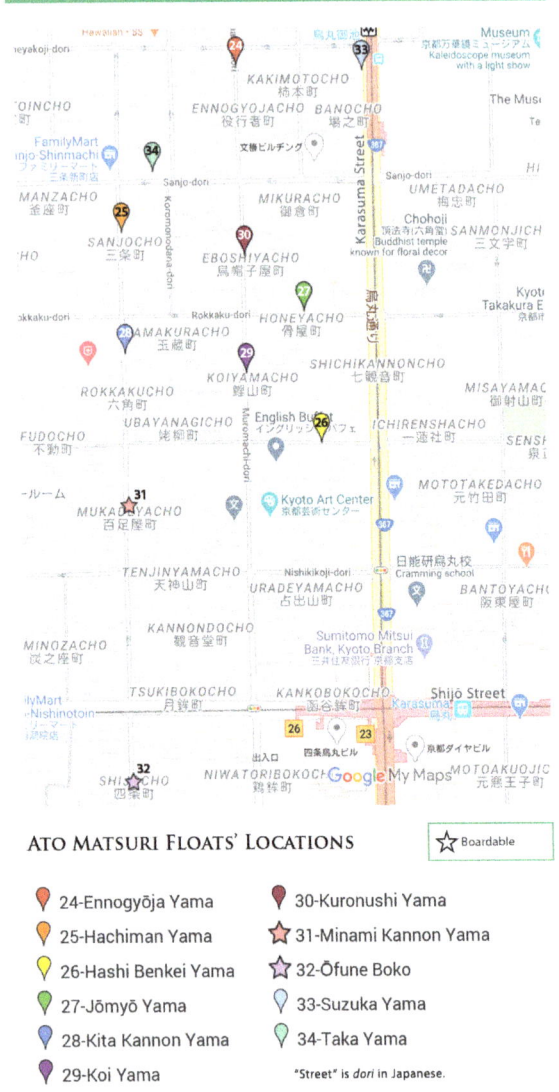

Ato Matsuri Floats' Locations ☆ Boardable

- 📍 24-Ennogyōja Yama
- 📍 25-Hachiman Yama
- 📍 26-Hashi Benkei Yama
- 📍 27-Jōmyō Yama
- 📍 28-Kita Kannon Yama
- 📍 29-Koi Yama
- 📍 30-Kuronushi Yama
- ☆ 31-Minami Kannon Yama
- ☆ 32-Ōfune Boko
- 📍 33-Suzuka Yama
- 📍 34-Taka Yama

"Street" is *dori* in Japanese.

Created by Catherine Pawasarat and Google Maps
Please visit GionFestival.org for my interactive maps.

Ato Matsuri Procession (7/24)

⛩ Otabisho

○ 8:15 Floats gather on Oike street, between Shinmachi and Karasuma.

◆ 9:30-10:30 Procession start, Karasuma Oike.

○ 9:40-10:40 Kuji Aratame, north side of Oike-Teramachi Intersection.

◇ 10:00-11:00 Tsuji Mawashi, Kawaramachi-Oike intersection.

◆ 10:40-11:40 Tsuji Mawashi, Kawaramachi-Shijō intersection.

◆ 11:20-12:20 End of floats procession, Karasuma-Shijō intersection.

Direction is clockwise. Times approximate.

"Street" is *dori* in Japanese.

Created by Catherine Pawasarat and Google Maps
Please visit GionFestival.org for my interactive maps.

Hanagasa Junko/Flower Umbrella Procession (7/24)

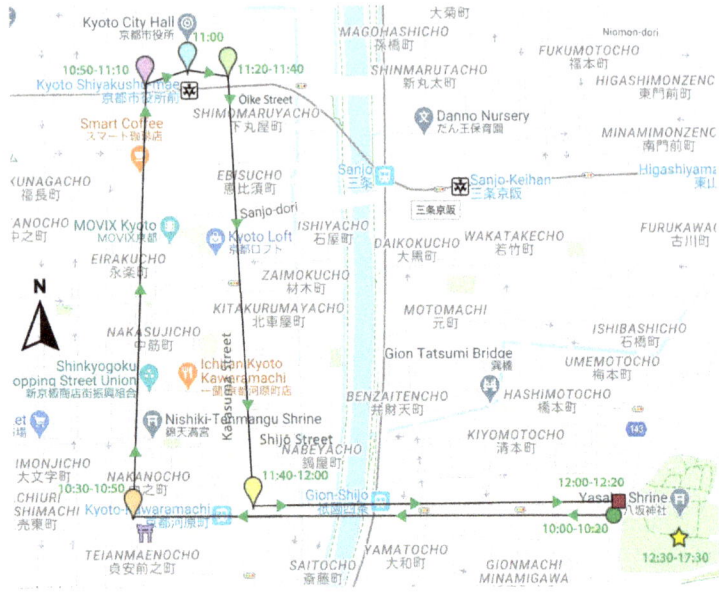

- Otabisho
- 10:00-10:20 Start from Yasaka Shrine, Higashiōji-Shijō intersection.
- 10:30-10:50 Teramachi Shijō intersection.
- 10:50-11:10 Teramachi Oike intersection.
- 11:00 City Hall.
- 11:20-11:40 Kawaramachi Oike intersection.
- 11:40-12:00 Kawaramachi Shijō intersection.
- 12:00-12:20 End at Yasaka Shrine.
- 12:30-17:30 Music and Dance after procession.

Route goes clockwise. Times approximate.

"Street" is *dori* in Japanese.

Created by Catherine Pawasarat and Google Maps
Please visit GionFestival.org for my interactive maps.

AFTERWORD

I moved to Kyoto from the U.S. in 1989 when I was 21. I lived there for about 20 years before moving to the British Columbia Rocky Mountains in western Canada to found and develop Clear Sky Meditation and Study Center with my partner and co-teacher Doug Duncan.

I'm a lover of language, and while in Kyoto I learned to speak and write Japanese. This has allowed me to develop friendships with locals in a way that many foreigners can't because of communication challenges. It also allowed me to delve much deeper into the fascinating mysteries of this ancient and cultured civilization. Truly the baths and cuisine are sublime!

I had the good fortune of being befriended by Higuchi Osamu, a kimono merchant who was my landlord when I moved into the Gion Festival's Kita Kannon Yama neighborhood. I was planning to head back to the U.S., but he introduced me to the world of Kyoto's traditional culture. It was worth staying for. In the 1990s, Kyoto's traditional culture was only open via personal introductions. It's thanks to Higuchi-san's generosity with his connections that I have so profoundly enjoyed my time in Kyoto.

Thanks to his introductions and mentorship, among other things I was able to study kyōgen theater with Living National Treasure Shigeyama Sensaku, and koto and shamisen in the Gion district with the wonderful musical artist Kōda Ritsuko. Living in that beautiful traditional home and garden in the heart of the Gion Festival neighborhood allowed me insights into the festival's past and the lives of people who have long supported it.

As rewarding as this time was, there was still something missing, and I began focusing on my spiritual practice. So I never really mastered these Japanese arts. But the exposure to traditional Japanese culture helped me understand the countless cultural aspects of the Gion Festival. My shamanistic and Buddhist meditation practices helped me connect with its deeper spiritual aspects.

My interest in the Gion Festival started very early in my time in Japan. Over the last 25 years, I was fortunate to develop friendships with many of the remarkable leaders and supporters of various floats. I feel honored that I've been able to record some of the festival elders' perspectives for posterity.

A few of my friends have asked me, "Catherine-san, where's your book?" I've been wanting to write this for many years. It brings me great joy now to offer this work to those many people who have helped me with countless conversations, interviews, tremendous hospitality, and general graciousness.

Each year the Gion Festival brings such a mix of strong feelings for me. There's excited anticipation at meeting my old friends and making new ones, wistful sorrow when I learn that people I cared about and respected passed away over the previous year, and joy in the appreciation of the preciousness of our time together. In truth this is what the Gion Festival and its anti-plague origins are all about: living, dying, and the richness of each moment in our short lives.

I hope this offering of my love for Japan, the Japanese people, and especially the Gion Festival and its dedicated community members will help repay some of the kindness, patience, and friendship they have shown me over the years.

本当に心から感謝申し上げます。
Hontō ni kokoro kara kansha mōshi agemasu.
I give my sincere and heartfelt thanks.

If you've enjoyed this book,
help grow generative travel by
leaving a review on
GoodReads.com or Amazon.com.

Learn more, stay in touch,
or contact the author via
GionFestival.org.